From Bullets to Ballots

In recent years, an increasing amount of research has argued that the successful transformation of rebel organization into parties is critical to stable post-conflict peace and democratization. However, the process of the transformation of rebel groups into parties is not well understood. Under what conditions do rebel groups transform into parties? Or into something else? What are the causal mechanisms that lead to the "successful" transformation of rebel groups into political parties? Does the transformation of rebel groups into parties actually contribute to political stability and democratization? How does transformation differ from region to region? The chapters in this book directly address these questions, and include a combination of broader theoretical and empirical chapters coupled with several in depth case studies by some of the most notable scholars in the field. It should prove indispensable to students of both civil wars, post-conflict peace, and political parties.

This book was originally published as a special issue of *Democratization*.

John Ishiyama is University Distinguished Research Professor of Political Science at the University of North Texas, USA. His research focuses on political institutions, democratization, and post–civil war politics.

Democratization Special Issues

Edited by
Jeffrey Haynes, *London Metropolitan University, UK*
Aurel Croissant, *University of Heidelberg, Germany*

The journal, *Democratization*, emerged in 1994, during 'the third wave of democracy', a period which saw democratic transformation of dozens of regimes around the world. Over the last decade or so, the journal has published a number of special issues as books, each of which has focused upon cutting edge issues linked to democratization. Collectively, they underline the capacity of democratization to induce debate, uncertainty, and perhaps progress towards better forms of politics, focused on the achievement of the democratic aspirations of men and women everywhere.

For a full list of titles please visit https://www.routledge.com/
Democratization-Special-Issues/book-series/DEM

Recent titles in this series include the following:

Religiously Oriented Parties and Democratization
Edited by Luca Ozzano and Francesco Cavatorta

Religion and Political Change in the Modern World
Edited by Jeffrey Haynes

Political Opposition in Sub-Saharan Africa
Edited by Elliott Green, Johanna Söderström and Emil Uddhammar

Conflicting Objectives in Democracy Promotion
Do all good things go together?
Edited by Julia Leininger, Sonja Grimm and Tina Freyburg

From Bullets to Ballots
Edited by John Ishiyama

From Bullets to Ballots
The Transformation of Rebel
Groups into Political Parties

Edited by
John Ishiyama

LONDON AND NEW YORK

First published 2018
by Routledge
2 Park Square, Milton Park, Abingdon, Oxon, OX14 4RN, UK

and by Routledge
711 Third Avenue, New York, NY 10017, USA

Routledge is an imprint of the Taylor & Francis Group, an informa business

© 2018 Taylor & Francis

All rights reserved. No part of this book may be reprinted or reproduced or utilised in any form or by any electronic, mechanical, or other means, now known or hereafter invented, including photocopying and recording, or in any information storage or retrieval system, without permission in writing from the publishers.

Trademark notice: Product or corporate names may be trademarks or registered trademarks, and are used only for identification and explanation without intent to infringe.

British Library Cataloguing in Publication Data
A catalogue record for this book is available from the British Library

ISBN 13: 978-1-138-08361-5

Typeset in Minion Pro
by diacriTech, Chennai

Publisher's Note
The publisher accepts responsibility for any inconsistencies that may have arisen during the conversion of this book from journal articles to book chapters, namely the possible inclusion of journal terminology.

Disclaimer
Every effort has been made to contact copyright holders for their permission to reprint material in this book. The publishers would be grateful to hear from any copyright holder who is not here acknowledged and will undertake to rectify any errors or omissions in future editions of this book.

Contents

Citation Information		vii
Notes on Contributors		ix

Introduction to the special issue "From bullets to ballots:
the transformation of rebel groups into political parties"
John Ishiyama — 1

1   Political party formation by former armed opposition
groups after civil war
Carrie Manning and Ian Smith — 4

2   Rebel-to-party transformations in civil war peace
processes 1975–2011
Mimmi Söderberg Kovacs and Sophia Hatz — 22

3   Does political inclusion of rebel parties promote
peace after civil conflict?
Michael Christopher Marshall and John Ishiyama — 41

4   From victorious rebels to strong authoritarian parties:
prospects for post-war democratization
Terrence Lyons — 58

5   The Guatemalan National Revolutionary unit: the long collapse — 74
Michael E. Allison

6   Rebel-to-political and back? Hamas as a security provider in Gaza
between rebellion, politics and governance
Benedetta Berti and Beatriz Gutiérrez — 91

Index — 109

Citation Information

The chapters in this book were originally published in *Democratization*, volume 23, issue 6 (October 2016). When citing this material, please use the original page numbering for each article, as follows:

Introduction

Introduction to the special issue "From bullets to ballots: the transformation of rebel groups into political parties"
John Ishiyama
Democratization, volume 23, issue 6 (October 2016) pp. 969–971

Chapter 1

Political party formation by former armed opposition groups after civil war
Carrie Manning and Ian Smith
Democratization, volume 23, issue 6 (October 2016) pp. 972–989

Chapter 2

Rebel-to-party transformations in civil war peace processes 1975–2011
Mimmi Söderberg Kovacs and Sophia Hatz
Democratization, volume 23, issue 6 (October 2016) pp. 990–1008

Chapter 3

Does political inclusion of rebel parties promote peace after civil conflict?
Michael Christopher Marshall and John Ishiyama
Democratization, volume 23, issue 6 (October 2016) pp. 1009–1025

Chapter 4

From victorious rebels to strong authoritarian parties: prospects for post-war democratization
Terrence Lyons
Democratization, volume 23, issue 6 (October 2016) pp. 1026–1041

CITATION INFORMATION

Chapter 5

The Guatemalan National Revolutionary unit: the long collapse
Michael E. Allison
Democratization, volume 23, issue 6 (October 2016) pp. 1042–1058

Chapter 6

Rebel-to-political and back? Hamas as a security provider in Gaza between rebellion, politics and governance
Benedetta Berti and Beatriz Gutiérrez
Democratization, volume 23, issue 6 (October 2016) pp. 1059–1076

For any permission-related enquiries please visit:
http://www.tandfonline.com/page/help/permissions

Notes on Contributors

Michael E. Allison is an Associate Professor of Political Science at the University of Scranton in Pennsylvania, USA.

Benedetta Berti is a Fellow at the Institute for National Security Studies (INSS), a Lecturer at Tel Aviv University, Israel, a TED Senior Fellow and a non-resident Senior Fellow at the Foreign Policy Research Institute (FPRI), USA.

Beatriz Gutiérrez is a former Researcher for Peace and International Security Studies at University Institute General Gutiérrez Mellado (IUGM), Spain.

Sophia Hatz is PhD candidate with the Department of Peace and Conflict Research, Uppsala University, Sweden.

John Ishiyama is University Distinguished Research Professor of Political Science at the University of North Texas, USA.

Terrence Lyons is an Associate Professor of Conflict Resolution at the School for Conflict Analysis and Resolution, George Mason University, USA, and Director of the doctoral programme.

Carrie Manning is Professor in the Department of Political Science, Georgia State University, USA.

Michael Christopher Marshall is a Visiting Assistant Professor at Miami University in Oxford Ohio, USA.

Ian Smith is a recent doctoral graduate of Georgia State University, USA.

Mimmi Söderberg Kovacs is Head of Research at the Folke Bernadotte Academy (FBA), Sweden.

Introduction to the special issue "From bullets to ballots: the transformation of rebel groups into political parties"

John Ishiyama

Department of Political Science, University of North Texas, Denton, TX, USA

ABSTRACT
In this special issue of *Democratization*, seven articles are presented that address the question of the transformation of armed rebel groups into political parties and what implications this transformation has on the development of post-conflict peace and democratization. The articles cover a wide variety of geographic cases, and use both quantitative and qualitative methods of inquiry.

In recent years, an increasing amount of research has emerged that has argued that the successful transformation of rebel organization into parties is critical to successful post-conflict peace and democratization.[1] Recent publications have explored how rebel groups have transformed themselves into political parties.[2] This new line of inquiry has evolved, in part, due to the realization that the creation of durable peace settlements requires the active involvement and cooperative engagement of these political groups. The transformation of rebel groups into political parties[3] provides channels for both interest articulation and political process engagement for former rebels, thus contributing to sustainable peace, stability, and democracy.[4] Indeed, as many point out, the peace duration after civil wars depends heavily on whether former rebel groups decide to adapt to, evade, or exit the post-war political arena.[5] In short, as Terrence Lyons points out, for parties to support the new political system and compete for power through ballots rather than bullets it is crucial to transform parties or those organizations made powerful by war into those capable of sustaining peace.[6]

However, the transformation process of rebel groups into parties is not well understood. Under what conditions do rebel groups transform into parties or into something else? What are the causal mechanisms that lead to the "successful" transformation of rebel groups into political parties? Does the transformation of rebel groups into parties actually contribute to political stability and democratization? Do these processes vary from country to country, or from region to region?

In this special issue of *Democratization*, the contributions address these questions. The first four articles tackle broader theoretical and empirical questions regarding the transformation of rebel groups into political parties. Carrie Manning and Ian Smith address the first question posed above. The authors use an original cross-national data set that extends from 1990 to 2009 and find that former armed opposition groups form political parties in more than half of the cases. What explains the successful transformations from rebel groups to political parties are the rebel group's pre-war political experience, the characteristics of the war, and the end of the conflict. However, they suggest that high rates of party formation by former armed opposition groups do not necessarily bode well for the development of democratically robust regimes. Sophia Hatz and Mimmi Söderberg Kovacs directly address the question of whether the provisions of a peace settlement that ends a civil war affect the likelihood of rebel-to-party transformation. Using data from 1975 to 2011 that covers both the characteristics of peace settlements and rebel-to-party outcomes, they find that the provisions in settlements that address rebel-to-party transformations do not by themselves explain rebel-to-party transformations. They suggest that other factors, beyond the specifics of peace settlements, may better explain rebel-to-party transformation. Michael Christopher Marshall and John Ishiyama focus on the *effects* of the transformation of rebel groups into political parties. They argue that the inclusion and participation of former rebel parties in national government has an important impact on the likelihood of post-settlement peace. In the fourth article, Terrence Lyons addresses the question of what happens to rebel groups that "won" a civil war – indeed, most work on the transformation process has examined groups emerging from civil war "settlements" or "agreements" rather than rebel victory. Using three cases from East Africa, Lyons finds that rebel victory leads to the transformation of rebel groups into authoritarian parties, which is why rebel victories are unlikely to lead to post-war democratization. Thus, strong authoritarian rule results from rebel victories in cases where wars ended in negotiated settlements, because rebel victories produce strong authoritarian parties.

The second set of articles examines important individual empirical cases of transformation. All point out the important effects of the organizational legacies of the war time experience on the ability of these rebel groups to transform into political parties. Michael Allison, unlike the other contributions, does not examine a "successful" transformation but an example of a "failed" case in Central America: the Guatemalan National Revolutionary Unit (URNG). He focuses on the organizational experiences of the URNG during the war, and argues that URNG's poor post-war electoral performance was caused by a combination of both internal organizational factors and institutional factors that characterized the post-war political system. Finally, Benedetta Berti and Beatriz Lopez examine how the Palestinian Hamas changed from an insurgent group to a "governing" party. In particular, they examine the important changes in the balance between the institutionalized security sector in Gaza (controlled by Hamas after it became a governing party in 2006) and the group's insurgent armed wing. This article points to an important aspect of the rebel-to-party transformation process: What happens to the armed wing of the group, once it becomes a political party? The answer to this question clearly has implications for both peace duration and post-conflict democratic development, not only in Gaza but also beyond.

In sum, the special issue covers some important new scholarship and offers new insights on the transformation of rebel groups into political parties. The special issue also provides broad geographic coverage of the topic. Thus, we believe this special issue will offer an important contribution to the literature on the process of organizational transformation and the building of peace and democracy after Civil Wars.

FROM BULLETS TO BALLOTS

Notes

1. Curtis and de Zeeuw, "Rebel Movements and Political Party Development"; de Zeeuw, *From Soldiers to Politicians*; Manning, "Armed Opposition Groups into Political Parties"; Manning, "Party-Building on the Heels of War."
2. de Zeeuw, *From Soldiers to Politicians*; Manning "Armed Opposition Groups into Political Parties."
3. Following Anthony Downs, political parties means a team of individuals running under a common label that seek office via a duly constituted election. The former rebel groups considered by this study clearly qualify as parties under this definition.
4. Ishiyama and Batta, "Swords into Plowshares"; de Zeeuw, *From Soldiers to Politicians*; Manning, "Armed Opposition Groups into Political Parties."
5. de Zeeuw, *From Soldiers to Politicians*; Manning, "Armed Opposition Groups into Political Parties"; Söderberg-Kovacs, *From Rebellion to Politics*.
6. Lyons, *Demilitarizing Politics*.

Disclosure statement

No potential conflict of interest was reported by the author.

Bibliography

Curtis, D., and Jeroun de Zeeuw. 2009. "Rebel Movements and Political Party Development in Post-Conflict Societies – A Short Literature Review." Accessed 25 May, 2015. http://www.statesandsecurity.org/_pdfs/CurtisZeeuw.pdf.

Downs, Anthony. *An Economic Theory of Democracy*. New York: Harper, 1957.

Ishiyama, John, and Anna Batta. "Swords into Plowshares: The Organizational Transformation of Rebel Groups into Political Parties." *Communist and Post Communist Studies* 44, no. 3 (2011): 369–379.

Lyons, Terrance. *Demilitarizing Politics: Elections on the Uncertain Road to Peace*. Boulder: Lynne Rienner, 2005.

Manning, Carrie. "Armed Opposition Groups into Political Parties: Comparing Bosnia, Kosovo and Mozambique." *Studies in Comparative International Development* 39, no. 2 (2004): 54–76.

Manning, Carrie. "Party-Building on the Heels of War: El Salvador, Bosnia, Kosovo and Mozambique." *Democratization* 14, no. 1 (2007): 1–25.

Söderberg- Kovacs, M. *From Rebellion to Politics*. Stockholm: Uppsala Universitet, 2007.

de Zeeuw, Jeroun. ed. 2007. *From Soldiers to Politicians: Transforming Rebel Movements after Civil War*. Boulder: Lynne Reinner, 2007.

RESEARCH ARTICLE

Political party formation by former armed opposition groups after civil war

Carrie Manning and Ian Smith

Department of Political Science, Georgia State University, Atlanta, Georgia, USA

ABSTRACT
Under what conditions are rebel groups successfully incorporated into democratic politics when civil war ends? Using an original cross-national, longitudinal dataset, we examine political party formation by armed opposition groups over a 20-year period, from 1990 to 2009. We find that former armed opposition groups form parties in more than half of our observations. A rebel group's pre-war political experience, characteristics of the war and how it ended outweigh factors such as the country's political and economic traits and history. We advance a theoretical framework based on rebel leaders' expectations of success in post-war politics, and we argue that high rates of party formation by former armed opposition groups are likely a reflection of democratic weakness rather than democratic robustness in countries emerging from conflict.

Introduction

The end of the Cold War presaged the end of many civil wars around the globe, with more such conflicts ending in the 15 years after 1989 than during 45 years of the Cold War.[1] Democratization has formed the cornerstone of most peace settlements in this period of "liberal peacebuilding," with the introduction or expansion of electoral politics providing an important and highly visible marker of the war to peace transition.[2] Liberal peacebuilding presumes that armed opposition groups will lay down their weapons and replace violent conflict with political competition. To what extent have armed opposition groups embraced this model?

This article presents a systematic exploration of the factors that influence whether or not an armed opposition group forms a political party following civil war. We constructed a cross-national, longitudinal dataset that tracks the incorporation of armed opposition groups into democratic politics after civil war over a 20-year period, from 1990 to 2009. We include conflicts that *ended* during this period; these include some that began as early as the 1960s and as late as 2009, bridging the Cold War and post-Cold War periods.

The dataset includes information on the characteristics of the armed conflict and the armed opposition groups, as well as on the characteristics of the post-war political system and the post-war electoral performance of former armed opposition groups.[3] Following Sartori, we define a political party as "any political group that presents at elections, and is capable of placing through elections, candidates for public office".[4] Party formation occurs when an armed opposition group registers as a legal party eligible to compete in elections.

The transformation of rebel groups into parties in no way guarantees either peace or democracy. When armed opposition groups register as legal political parties they are taking the necessary first step toward accepting political competition as a substitute, or at least a supplement, to violence as a route to political power.

A growing literature explores the transition of armed opposition groups – including both terrorist organizations and rebel groups – to political parties.[5] Most of these are empirically rich single case or small-n comparative studies focusing on a handful of key cases, and they have yielded important insights that deserve further exploration.

This project seeks to build on that base. Our independent variables are drawn from it and from the vast literature on party development, civil wars and post-war politics. A survey of this literature suggests possible correlations between post-rebel party formation and pre-war political experience of the rebel group; conflict intensity and duration; how the war ended; and the political and economic environment at war's end.

In the section that follows, we construct hypotheses about these relationships that we then test against our data. We find that rebel groups form parties more often than not (54.8% of the time). Rebel groups with pre-war political and especially electoral experience are significantly more likely to form parties and that both comprehensive and partial peace agreements make post-rebel party formation more likely. We also find that more violent conflicts reduce the likelihood that rebel groups will form parties after the war. Variables relating to the post-war political and economic environment were not significant, an unexpected and intriguing result.

Our results must be interpreted with caution. Large-n comparative research on post-conflict politics presents a number of challenges, including multicollinearity, potentially complex interactions and considerable variation across a relatively small number of country cases. While most statistical treatments assume that independent variables are largely independent of one another, we know that empirically the variables we identify are linked to one another in complex ways, and the impact of one factor is likely to be contingent on the presence of others.

For example, a negotiated peace might give warring parties that participate in negotiations opportunities to shape post-war democratic institutions in ways beneficial to themselves. A country's pre-war experience with democracy might also affect the specific types of democratic institutions that are created in the post-war period. The intensity of the war, the history of pre-war politics and the nature of the peace settlement might all affect the confidence of party leaders in the durability and reliability of post-war institutions, thus affecting their calculations regarding the value of participating in politics.

One of the goals of this paper is to tease out these relationships in order to contribute to theory building in this area. Though our aim is primarily theory-building rather than theory testing, we do explore the explanatory power of competing explanations. In the absence of clear theoretical reasons to privilege one set of explanations over another, we give equal weight to each of the competing arguments we present.

Understanding post-war political incorporation of armed groups

The literatures on party development, political transition and civil war suggest that factors related to party history, war characteristics, the war to peace transition and the post-war political environment might be expected to influence post-rebel party formation.[6] In this section we construct hypotheses about these relationships, which we then test against our data. Our inquiry begins with two assumptions, both drawn from the comparative literature on party organization and development. First, rebel groups and political parties are not unitary actors but, as Sartori has argued about parties, both are comprised of sub-groups whose membership and interests may shift over time. These sub-groups might be based on deeply rooted ideological differences or on differences over tactics or strategy arising from the functional role of some sub-groups over others.[7]

Second, like most organizations, rebel groups and political parties seek both to achieve particular goals and to sustain themselves as organizations.[8] Their leaders face a similar dual task as they seek to maintain their leadership positions and preserve the organization itself. These goals are sometimes in tension with one another. We hypothesize that leaders will make decisions about whether or not to form a party and participate in post-war electoral politics based on whether or not doing so threatens or bolsters the survival of their organization, their leadership role in the organization, or both.

Party history

The case for considering a party's prior political experience is straightforward. If an armed opposition group was a political party prior to the war, it might have a level of organizational structure and coherence, as well as experienced political cadres and a collective identity, that could help sustain it in post-war politics.[9] In the face of the very different set of challenges posed by democratic politics, compared to military imperatives, such organizations may be more resilient. There is considerable evidence in the broader comparative literature that parties that played a substantial role in the period preceding the transition to democracy tend to predominate afterwards, unless they are formally banned from participation in politics.[10] For example, the literature on successor parties in the former Soviet bloc and in post-authoritarian regimes in Africa suggests that successor parties have proven quite durable.[11] To explore whether parties with prior experience as political organizations do better than those that first came into existence as armed opposition groups, we code whether a rebel group had existed as a political party immediately prior to the outbreak of war.

Of course, this is a simplification of a complex reality. Rebel groups that were pre-war parties differ from one another in important ways. Some were narrowly based while others were broad fronts; their social bases differed, as did the competitiveness of the political environment they faced and the rules and tools of competition. Organizational characteristics – how centralized and how institutionalized the party was – are also likely to be relevant.[12] Some used violence as an ancillary strategy, some did not. Nevertheless, as a first cut it is worth grouping together armed opposition groups (AOGs) with a past organizational life in politics as a group distinct from those that were formed as rebel groups per se. As much of the broader comparative party literature has established, an organization's past is likely to affect its future. Pre-war experience as a party creates human and organizational capital that can be useful in forming a new party.[13]

Similarly, we expect that parties with pre-war experience in *electoral* environments are likely to perform even better in post-war electoral politics than those with non-electoral political experience. Adjusting to the challenges of electoral politics should be easier for parties that have previously had to develop decision-making mechanisms to select candidates, to adjudicate between competing ideas about party platform and to maintain a voting base. Indeed, De Zeeuw and his contributors find that past experience with democracy is an asset to rebel groups in the transition to party politics.[14] We thus code parties according to whether or not they competed in elections prior to the post-war period. Both this variable and prior political experience are dummy variables.

War legacies

Where the literature on post-Communist successor parties focuses on the historical legacy of Communist rule, the post-conflict literature explores the implications of the war itself for post-war party development.[15] Finding theoretical guidance for this question is challenging. Much of the literature is focused on peace as an outcome. While certainly peace, at least in the short term, is essential for the creation of an electoral infrastructure that would incentivize and mobilize party formation by rebel groups, the wartime characteristics require further exploration in order to yield useful hypotheses on party formation, as we discuss below. New work is beginning to explore the impact of civil war on democracy and its component parts.[16] Findings are mixed. For example, Fortna and Huang find that for the most part "characteristics of the civil war have relatively little effect on the prospects for post-war democratization".[17] Drilling down from democracy to party system, Ishiyama finds that conflict intensity does have a significant impact, with more intensive conflicts leading to dominant-party systems.[18]

The war characteristics examined in our analysis are conflict duration and conflict intensity (battle deaths). These variables are drawn from the Uppsala Conflict Data Program (UCDP) Conflict Termination and PRIO Battle-Related Deaths datasets.[19] Intensity is coded as the sum of battle deaths for a conflict episode based on estimates from the UCDP interval data on battle deaths.[20] We code conflict duration in months based on the start and end dates provided in the UCDP data. Other war-related characteristics, such as the wartime strategies of combatant groups, rebel groups' finance arrangements and support from external sponsors, would also be worth investigating for their impact on post-rebel party formation. Better data on these characteristics is now emerging from new case studies and small-*n* comparative work, allowing future research to build useful variables for some of these factors.[21] However, it remains difficult to collect accurate data on these variables for the full range of cases, and here we have opted to use battle deaths and duration as a first cut.

To understand the possible impact of war duration and intensity on post-conflict politics, we can start by building on the findings of the conflict recurrence literature, though the implications of those findings for post-rebel party formation might be quite different than they are for conflict recurrence. For example, there is considerable evidence that higher intensity wars – those that cause high numbers of deaths and large-scale displacement – are less likely to be followed by lasting peace.[22] One reason for this might be that more intense wars entrench wartime cleavages that are hard to overcome.

But the creation of entrenched wartime cleavages might actually improve the chances that an armed opposition group decides to form a party, since strong cleavages may increase cohesion within the parties on either side, and the ability to count on a clearly identified popular base would likely improve the party's electoral performance.[23] Ishiyama's finding that "bloodier civil wars promote the emergence of dominant-party systems with reduced electoral volatility" may offer support for the hypothesis that intense wars freeze wartime cleavages.[24]

On the other hand, it is important to consider how violence has been used. Battle deaths may be a function of rebel or government strategy and tactics, of the "technology of violence" and the degree to which conflict is asymmetrical, since weaker groups may use more violence as a force magnifier. Without knowing who were the victims of violence and the relationship of those victims to different belligerents in the conflict, it is difficult to interpret the substantive impact of the correlation between battle deaths and party formation. We do not explore this intermediate relationship between violence and cleavage structures in this dataset, but it is worth examining in future research. For now, we simply offer an exploration of the relationship between battle deaths and party formation as a first cut on which to build a more nuanced investigation. We hypothesize that more violent conflicts are more likely to produce post-rebel party formation, because they are more likely to entrench cleavages around which parties could mobilize votes. Mobilization on each side might result from positive support for a side, or from security calculations that dictate cooperation in exchange for survival.[25]

Since duration is closely related to other factors such as battle deaths, it is difficult to isolate its effects. However, we hypothesize that longer wars should produce a higher likelihood of post-rebel party formation for three reasons. First, long wars, like high intensity wars, may produce more entrenched cleavage structures that could prove advantageous in electoral politics. Second, longer wars may allow time for armed opposition groups to develop a more coherent organizational structure or collective identity. Third, though mutual distrust between belligerents may be greater in the wake of a long war, potential spoilers looking for a return to war may face more resistance from war-weary civilians, and may decide that forming a party and playing the electoral game is the path of least resistance. This is consistent with the "war weariness" thesis found in the literature on duration and conflict recurrence.[26] In sum, we expect that more intense conflicts, and longer conflicts, are more likely to result in post-rebel party formation.

War to peace transition

De Zeeuw and his contributors find that "perhaps the most important exogenous factor impacting rebel-to-party transformation is the extent to which the civil war has ended".[27] Wars that have come to a definitive end, and more specifically those that have ended in a peace agreement, are more conducive to rebel to party transformations. This is consistent with Doyle and Sambanis who, among others, argue that a peace agreement significantly boosts the chances of "participatory peace" after civil war.[28] Fortna and Huang find that negotiated settlements have a positive impact on post-war democratization, but only in the short term (2–5 years).[29]

Just as a peace agreement is expected to increase the chances of successful transition from battlefield to political arena for armed opposition groups, a military victory by government is expected to hurt the chances of such a transition. In the case of military victory by the government, repression of opposition is not uncommon, and formal provision is less likely to be made for the rebel to party transformation. We would thus expect post-rebel party formation to be less likely in such cases. In the case of military victory by rebels, on the other hand, if the post-war political system is based on elections, we would expect to see such groups form parties and participate in elections.

Another possible outcome of civil war is a "separate peace", in which a peace agreement is signed that leaves one or more armed opposition groups still fighting. We theorize that even such a partial peace provides an incentive to the rebel groups included in the agreement to form parties and participate in politics in order both to maximize their chances of gaining a share of the political spoils and to distinguish themselves from insurgent groups still fighting. Indeed, we might expect such groups to be more likely to form parties than rebel groups subject to a comprehensive peace. Groups willing to negotiate a separate peace might have done so in part because they calculated that their chances of survival were better in the political arena than on the battlefield, and they may even have negotiated guarantees of their ability to participate in politics.

In sum, we expect that, all else equal, armed opposition groups are more likely to form parties when war ends in some sort of a negotiated peace agreement, whether comprehensive or "separate". Where there is provision for democratic post-war politics, military victory by the rebel group should also be conducive to party formation and persistence.

Post-war environment

The post-war institutional structure might well affect party formation. We explore the influence of post-war institutional incentives by examining both political openness at the end of the conflict and whether the electoral system is proportional vs. majoritarian. We assume that electoral systems based on proportional representation offer a greater promise of success for new parties, since entry barriers are lower. We code these as "permissive" electoral systems. Similarly, more open systems promise parties that contest elections greater assurance that the results of the poll will both reflect the will of the electorate and will be implemented. We code openness of the political system in terms of Freedom House political rights scores.

Finally, some scholars argue that structural conditions in the pre-war, wartime or post-war periods shape both the party and the political environment in which that party operates. These conditions are both beyond the reach of institutional design and independent of the organizational capacities or motivations of armed opposition groups. For example, pre-existing socioeconomic, political or cultural cleavages may continue to define the post-war political system and its dominant political actors. After the war, socioeconomic factors such as level and rate of economic growth, or regional economic inequalities, may impact the expected and actual performance of political parties, including post-rebel parties. In addition, the presence of armed conflict in neighbouring states, or the existence of "safe havens" or other exit strategies for would-be spoilers, might also affect the decisions of rebel leaders about whether or not to form a political party and under what circumstances to participate. We include controls for region, level of economic development and past history of democracy in the country. However, in this iteration we do not control for conflict in neighbouring countries or other factors related to the post-war security environment.

Exploring the data

The dataset

Our dataset builds on the UCDP Conflict Termination and Actors datasets. It covers all intrastate conflict episodes ending and holding post-war elections between 1990 and 2009 and includes conflicts in 50 countries. Using these criteria, we coded 98 unique conflict episodes and identified 133 distinct armed opposition groups.[30] In our dataset, a single observation is an AOG-conflict episode, yielding 155 observations.[31] In 19 conflict episodes, armed opposition groups returned to fighting before the first post-conflict election. Armed opposition groups that returned to war before elections were held may have done so after calculating that they could not succeed politically, so it was important to include them in the dataset. However, we also want to know how many groups that do not return to conflict also do not decide to form parties or participate in electoral politics. When we exclude observations of groups that went back to fighting before the first election from the analysis, we get the same number of conflict-episodes and countries, but a smaller number of AOG-conflict episodes to 136 observations of 127 distinct rebel groups. We ran a separate analysis of these cases, but there was little difference from the full set thus the smaller set is not included below. Appendix 1 contains the list of countries, AOGs and parties in the dataset.

Our dependent variable, post-rebel party formation, is defined as whether a former armed opposition group that fought in the most recent conflict episode formed a legal political party. Our key independent variables relate to pre-war political experience; war characteristics; how the war ended; and post-war political characteristics. Table 1 provides a list of independent variables, definitions and sources.

Coding for this project presented some challenges. First, as other scholars have observed, AOGs with pre-war experience as political parties vary widely in the nature and length of that experience and in their organizational coherence and structure, as well as in their approach to the use of violence prior to the beginning of the conflict.[32] Our set includes well-institutionalized parties with decades of experience, personalized "cliques of notables," loosely organized fronts and everything in between. AOGs in the set reflect similar diversity. Prior electoral experience means the party participated in elections, regardless of how free and fair those elections might have been. Future studies could refine coding of parties' prior organizational experience to account more directly for organizational and ideational capital that post-rebel parties might inherit from a previous political incarnation.

We looked for post-war party formation in every post-war election, so we include parties that formed to contest elections immediately as well as those that formed later on. Patterns of politics that led to and followed war varied widely, from cases in which armed groups cycled into politics and back to the battlefield with some regularity, to those that followed a more linear path. Some armed opposition groups produced a single party that proved durable (UNITA, Renamo), while in other cases AOGs formed multiple parties at the first elections. Sometimes several rebel groups united to form a single party after the war (Democratic Republic of Congo).

Rebel groups are not the only organizations that use violence. Political parties may have armed wings or youth militias. In some post-conflict countries, violence around elections, by groups associated with particular parties, may be seen by these parties as politics as normal, rather than as armed opposition activity. Our definition of

FROM BULLETS TO BALLOTS

Table 1. Hypotheses, definitions, sources.

DV: Political party formation: Was a legal political party formed after the conflict episode?
Sources: Nohlen et al. 2001; Nohlen et al. 1999; Nohlen 2005; Europa Regional Yearbooks
H1: Prior experience as a political party makes post-rebel party formation more likely.
IV: Did rebel group emerge from a political party formed before start of war?
Sources: UCDP Actor Dataset v. 2.1–2012; Nohlen et al. 2001; Nohlen et al. 1999; Nohlen 2005; Regional Yearbooks
H2: Prior experience as an electoral political party makes post-rebel party formation more likely.
IV: Did rebel group emerge from a political party that had contested elections before the start of the war?
Sources: UCDP Actor Dataset v. 2.1–2012; Nohlen et al. 2001; Nohlen et al. 1999; Nohlen 2005; Europa Regional
  Yearbooks
H3: Higher intensity conflict increases chances of post-rebel party formation.
IV: Interval data on battle deaths
Sources: PRIO Battle Deaths Dataset v. 3, presented in Lacina and Gleditsch 2005
H4: Longer conflicts increase the chances of post-rebel party formation.
IV: Duration of conflict, measured in months
Sources: UCDP/PRIO Armed Conflict Dataset, presented in Themner and Wallensteen 2014
H5: Presence of a general peace agreement increases the chances of post-rebel party formation.
IV: Peace agreement signed by all parties to the conflict
Sources: UCDP Conflict Termination Dataset v.2010–1, 1946–2009, Presented in Kreutz 2010
H6: Presence of a partial agreement increases the chances of post-rebel party formation.
IV: At least one peace agreement signed by some rebel groups while others continued to fight
Sources: USIP database of peace agreements; UCDP Conflict Termination Dataset v.2010–1, 1946–2009
H7: Military victory by government decreases chances of post-rebel party formation.
IV: Military victory by government
Source: UCDP Conflict Termination Dataset v.2010–1, 1946–2009; Europa Regional yearbooks.
H8: Military victory by rebels increases chances of post-rebel party formation.
IV: Military victory by rebels
Source: UCDP Conflict Termination Dataset v.2010–1, 1946–2009; Europa Regional Yearbooks
H9: Higher levels of political openness increase likelihood of post-rebel party formation.
IV: Freedom House Political Rights score
Source: Freedom House data, available at https://freedomhouse.org/report/freedom-world-aggregate-and-
  subcategory-scores
H10: More permissive rules of political competition increases likelihood of post-rebel party formation.
IV: PR electoral system
Sources: Nohlen et al. 2001; Nohlen et al. 1999; Nohlen 2005; Europa Regional Yearbooks
H11: International supervision of peace implementation increases likelihood of party formation.
IV: Multilateral peace operation in place Contact group or other committee of bilateral actors oversees
  implementation
Source: UCDP Peace Agreement dataset v. 2.0, 1975–2011, presented in Harbom et al. 2006; Hogbladh 2011
Controls: Geographic region; past history of democratic governance.
Sources: Economic development (GDP/capita) – Penn World Tables PWT 6.3 https://pwt.sas.upenn.edu/, presented
  in Heston et al. 2009; Freedom House aggregate scores

political party accommodates this possibility. For the purposes of this study, an AOG becomes a political party when it registers as a legal party and runs in its first election; a party is an organization that presents candidates for election and strives, as its primary goal, to place its candidates in office. If violence remains an ancillary strategy to achieving this goal, it does not necessarily disqualify an organization as a party (Table 2).

Data analysis: post-rebel party formation

To analyse our data, we use a logit model, as our dependent variable is a simple dichotomous option of whether a party forms or not. Each case in this model refers to the end of a conflict episode reported in the UCDP Actors dataset that was followed by some form of elections during the observation period between 1990 and 2009. A party was formed in 54.8% of the cases.

FROM BULLETS TO BALLOTS

Table 2. Descriptive statistics.

Variable	Mean/proportion	Min	Max
Party Formed	54.8%	0	1
Pre-war Electoral Party	11.6%	0	1
Pre-war Non-electoral Party	9.0%	0	1
Separate Peace	18.7%	0	1
General Peace	34.8%	0	1
Inactivity	40.0%	0	1
AOG Victory	7.1%	0	1
AOG Defeat	6.5%	0	1
Secessionist	35.5%	0	1
Battle Deaths	99,920.91	35	804,073
Conflict Duration (Year)	7.81	0.08	31.67
Cold War Era	34.2%	0	1
Permissive Elections	37.4%	0	1
Political Rights (FH)	5.08	1	7
Pre-war Multiparty Elections (within 10 years)	62.6%	0	1
Election Delay	3.35	0	19
Peacekeeping Operation	16.1%	0	1
External Implementation	20.6%	0	1
Domestic Implementation	6.5%	0	1
Europe	9.0%	0	1
Asia	25.2%	0	1
Americas	4.5%	0	1
Mideast	5.8%	0	1
Observations:	155		

We used multiple model specifications to examine multivariate correlations between a number of independent variables culled from the literature. The models were robust to changes in specifications, with only very slight changes between specifications. The models shown are estimates using clustered standard errors based on country-level factors, but the results were not significantly different when standard errors were clustered on conflict episodes or when non-clustered errors were utilized.[33] We also ran a simplified second model in which variables with little impact on the overall model fit were removed.[34] This second model is used to generate substantive statistics from the estimates.

The multivariate model is intended primarily as an exploratory analysis. This brings two cautions to bear. The first concerns the large number of variables. With so many variables it is likely that there are complex interactions between them, which will need to be accounted for in causal models developed from this analysis. Second, since this is an exploratory analysis of new data, we look not only at what is "confirmed" but also at those values that are close to significance, using graphical representations.[35] The largely heuristic nature of our analysis leads us to be concerned both with statistical consistency and with the substantive impact on party formation, which may be of greater value to consumers of political research. Table 3 presents the results of our logit model. Figure 1 provides a graphical interpretation of the substantive impact of the key dichotomous independent variables. It shows the average marginal effects calculated for a change from 0 to 1 for each.[36] For each one, the other variables are held to their mean value. (Estimates for political rights and battle deaths, our continuous variables, are not shown in the figure.)

12

FROM BULLETS TO BALLOTS

Table 3. Party formation: logit model.

	Model 1			Model 2		
Variable	Coef. Est.	R.S.E.	$P \geq |z|$	Coef. Est.	R.S.E.	$P \geq |z|$
Pre-war Electoral Party	3.449	0.995	0.001	3.435	1.042	0.001
Pre-war Non-electoral Party	1.702	0.920	0.064	1.586	0.736	0.031
Separate Peace	1.882	0.480	0.000	1.816	0.474	0.000
Inactivity	−1.732	0.470	0.000	−1.882	0.437	0.000
AOG Victory	0.973	1.420	0.493			
AOG Defeat	−2.390	1.019	0.019	−2.599	0.960	0.007
Secessionist Conflict	−1.194	0.924	0.196	−1.373	0.962	0.153
Battle Deaths (10,000)	−0.071	0.021	0.001	−0.060	0.018	0.001
Duration (Years)	0.017	0.047	0.722			
Cold War	1.634	0.624	0.009	1.776	0.595	0.003
Permissive Elections	−1.174	0.561	0.036	−0.988	0.534	0.064
Political Rights (FH)	0.380	0.198	0.055	0.330	0.164	0.044
Recent Multiparty Elections	−1.134	0.547	0.038	−1.171	0.552	0.034
Election Delay	−0.010	0.092	0.909			
Peacekeeping Operation	−0.100	0.771	0.897			
External Implementation	1.851	0.716	0.010	1.755	0.555	0.002
Domestic Implementation	−0.342	0.849	0.687			
Europe	1.830	0.880	0.037	1.797	0.890	0.044
Asia	2.015	0.887	0.023	2.107	0.964	0.029
Americas	0.669	1.753	0.703			
Mideast	3.303	1.321	0.012	3.290	1.476	0.026
Constant	−1.432	1.120	0.201	−1.041	1.042	0.317
N	155			155		
Wald X^2	142.61			112.04		
$P \geq X^2$	0.000			0.000		
AIC	173.53			167.93		

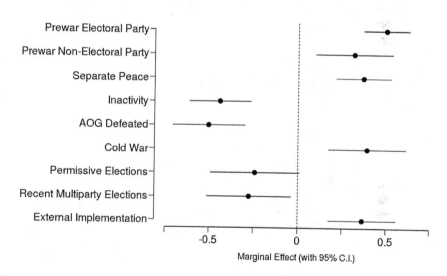

Figure 1. Marginal effects of binary variables.

Analysis

In both specifications of the model, we find variables from each of our conceptual areas to be influential. Consistent with our expectations, prior party experience, both electoral and non-electoral, was important. Whether or not a rebel group had a pre-war incarnation as

FROM BULLETS TO BALLOTS

an electoral party was consistently the most statistically and substantively significant variable in our model. Experience as a party, but not an electoral party, prior to the conflict episode is statistically significant at the 90% level in both specifications, but is not as influential as pre-war electoral experience.

Our findings regarding the post-war political environment were most surprising. We expected party formation to be more likely in more open political systems and where electoral rules meant lower barriers to entry. Instead, we found that AOGs were actually less likely to form parties in proportional representation systems than in those that utilized single-member systems. And parties formed from AOGs more often in countries where respect for political rights was lower (as measured by Freedom House scores).

These findings suggest that rebel leaders' decisions about party formation were not heavily influenced by calculations of their likely electoral success. If they were, we might expect to see higher rates of party formation in countries with a higher level of democratic openness (where new parties could expect a level playing field), or in cases with PR electoral systems (coded as "permissive"), where the barriers to entry for elected office would be lower. Perhaps merely participating in elections has instrumental value to these groups, even if the outcome is not electoral victory.

Alternatively, our assumption that proportional electoral systems mean lower barriers to office may be inaccurate for rebel groups. In fact, single member districts may well benefit rebels more, particularly if they have a territorial base that they controlled during wartime. Ishiyama also finds that electoral systems have different effects in post-war cases, noting that, unlike in other new democracies "these institutional factors had no effect on party systems characteristics among countries that had experienced a civil war".[37] We also found that in countries where there had been a multiparty election within 10 years of the start of the conflict episode (coded as "recent multiparty elections"), armed opposition groups were significantly *less* likely to form political parties. It may be that older, pre-war parties are able to crowd out newer entrants, including post-rebel parties. However, this finding must be interpreted with caution. First, the holding of pre-war elections tells us nothing about the age of the party system or of the dominant parties therein. Moreover, 10 years is a relatively broad time-span, and the quality of these pre-war elections varied considerably.

It is not surprising that AOGs with prior electoral experience are more likely to form post-rebel parties. Perhaps the polarizing effects of war reinforce or create entrenched cleavages that define the post-war party system regardless of post-war institutions.

But why should prior electoral experience matter when the likelihood of a level playing field appears unimportant? One possible answer is that parties with electoral experience might understand that electoral victory matters less than participation itself. The ability to field candidates for office is important even if electoral outcomes are not, as participation in elections allows groups to demonstrate their potential importance as allies or power-brokers even if they earn relatively small vote shares. For example, a party may use an election to demonstrate that it has deep support in a strategic region of the country, or that it has the support of a particular socioeconomic sector. Parties with prior electoral experience are likely to make a better showing regardless of how meaningful elections are. An alternative answer is that parties with prior electoral experience may be better positioned to manipulate electoral processes than those who have never contested an election.

Method of war termination had a significant and substantive impact on party formation. In our analysis, we use general peace agreement as the omitted reference category. Our first finding is that armed opposition groups that make a separate peace with the government are also more likely to form parties. This is not surprising, since parties that negotiate a separate peace are more likely to do so if they expect to survive the transition from battlefield to political arena. Not surprisingly, conflicts that end with the defeat of the rebel group by government forces or due to inactivity on the battlefield are less likely to lead to party formation. Wars ended through government victory or inactivity likely offer few if any assurances to rebel groups regarding their chances of survival in the political arenas.

Rebel victories were not significantly more likely to lead to party formation than a general peace agreement. This was counter to our expectations. The number of cases in this category is relatively small, so it is difficult to generalize. But the literature on organizational change would suggest that parties, like other organizations, adapt only when necessary to achieve their goals: political power, survival or policy change. Victorious rebel groups may have little reason to make the transition to party.[38]

Measures of the intensity and duration of the conflict had differing impacts. Contrary to our expectations, more intense conflicts significantly *reduce* the likelihood that armed opposition groups make the transition to political parties. However, our measure of intensity (battle deaths) does not allow us to make distinctions about the targets and types of violence, both of which might affect the impact on cleavage formation and rebel groups' expectations about popular support after the war. And violence might itself be a reflection of the strengths and weaknesses of rebel groups.[39] Finally, higher levels of wartime violence (and longer wars) might be a function of government preferences regarding whether and when to attempt negotiated peace.

War duration had no significant impact in the first model shown and was dropped due to a high degree of collinearity with the indicator variable for Cold War era conflicts. Party formation was significantly more likely in Cold War era conflicts (those that began before 1990). These conflicts frequently involved more ideologically-focused combatants with a greater degree of external support. This degree of organization and financial support provides a base upon which to build a party. Also, such conflicts were almost all ended through a negotiated peace agreement overseen by Western donors and/or multilateral organizations. In such conflicts, the barriers to new party formation were extremely low, as provisions for participation by ex-belligerents were often written into the peace agreement, and the opportunity cost of not forming a party was high. In such cases, party formation was the price of admission to both formal and informal struggles for power and resources.

In light of this possibility, we decided to test the influence of external involvement in the supervision of peace processes more directly. Interestingly, we found that the presence of a peacekeeping mission per se had no meaningful impact on party formation by AOGs. However, if external involvement included a committee of donors to oversee the agreement, party formation was significantly more likely. When supervision committees included only domestic actors, there was no notable impact on party formation. Recent research has shown that bilateral actors like major donors can be more effective than multilateral peacekeeping operations in exercising conditionality in peacebuilding processes.[40] These findings suggest that these actors likely provide carrots and/or sticks that affect the calculations of armed opposition groups regarding party formation after war.

Conclusion

This article has examined the question of when and why rebel groups form political parties at war's end. We theorized at the outset that rebel leaders would establish parties when they believed that doing so would contribute to their goal of organizational survival and retention of their leadership positions within the organization. In other words, parties would form where the barriers to success are low, and/or where the opportunity costs of not forming a party are high. Our findings offer some support to this theory. We found that parties were especially likely to form: when rebel groups had prior political and especially electoral experience; when there was a peace agreement, and especially where rebels signed a "separate peace" with the government; and when external guarantors were present. These factors likely increase rebel leaders' confidence in their ability to compete and survive in the post-war system. Interestingly, post-war political openness did not affect the chances of party formation. This suggests that post-rebel party formation may have little to do with a party's expectations of electoral success in free and fair elections. Participation in flawed elections may be sufficient for AOGs to reap the expected benefits. Where democratic institutions are weak, as in many post-conflict countries, where there are few strong political challengers to the former belligerents, or where the participation of the rebels is viewed by donors or other influential actors to be important to peace, the risks associated with the transition from rebel group to party are reduced, and the opportunity costs of not participating in elections increase, regardless of whether the party is winning or losing.

Disclosure statement

No potential conflict of interest was reported by the authors.

Notes

1. Flores and Nooruddin, "The Effects of Elections"; Kreutz, *How and When Armed Conflicts End*.
2. Dudouet et al., *From Combatants to Peacebuilders*; Paris, *At War's End*; United States Institute of Peace, *Guiding Principles*; Zuercher et al., *Costly Democracy*.
3. The dataset also contains information on party performance and persistence. We find that the majority of AOGs form parties and compete in elections over an extended period of time. This is particularly interesting given the considerable diversity of the AOGs, conflicts, and countries included in the dataset. However, we leave analysis of performance and persistence to a future project.
4. Sartori, *Parties and Party Systems*, 56.
5. Allison, "The Legacy of Violence"; Allison, "The Transition from Armed Opposition"; Altier et al., "Violence, Elections, and Party Politics"; Curtis, "Transitional Governance"; Curtis and de Zeeuw, "Rebel Movements" "; De Zeeuw, *Soldiers into Politicians*; De Zeeuw, *Political Party Development*; Deonandan et al., *Revolutionary Movements to Political Parties*; Garibay, "De La Lutte Armee"; Ishiyama and Batta, "Swords into Plowshares"; Manning, *Making of Democrats*; Ogura, "Seeking State Power"; Porto et al., *From Soldiers to Citizens*; Soderberg Kovacs, "When Rebels Change."
6. See Bratton and van de Walle, *Democratic Experiments in Africa*; Fortna and Huang, "Democratization after Civil War"; ; Ishiyama "Civil Wars and Party Systems"; Ishiyama, "The Sickle or the Rose"; Kitschelt et al., *Post-Communist Party Systems*; Manning, *Making of Democrats*; Manning, "Party-Building on Heels of War"; Panebianco, *Political Parties*; Reilly and Nordlund, *Political Parties*; Smith, "Former Sole Legal Party Performance"; Zuercher et al., *Costly Democracy*.
7. Panebianco, *Political Parties*; Sartori, *Parties and Party Systerms*.

FROM BULLETS TO BALLOTS

8. Panebianco, *Political Parties*.
9. Ishiyama, "Communist Parties"; Ishiyama, "The Sickle or the Rose"; Ishiyama and Batta, "Swords into Plowshares."
10. Ishiyama, "Sickle or Rose"; Ishiyama, "Communist Parties"; Ishiyama, "Party Organization"; Manning, "Party-Building on Heels of War"; Smith, "Former Sole Legal Party Performance."
11. Ishiyama, "Communist Parties"; Ishiyama, "Sickle or Rose?"; Smith, "Former Sole Legal Parties."
12. Bratton and van de Walle, *Democratic Experiments in Africa*; Ishiyama, "Sickle or Rose?"; Kitschelt et al., *Post-Communist Party Systems*; Manning, *Making of Democrats*.
13. Ishiyama, "Communist Parties"; Ishiyama, "Sickle or Rose?"; Ishiyama and Batta, "Swords into Plowshares"; Panebianco, *Political Parties*; Reilly and Nordlund, *Political Parties*.
14. De Zeeuw, *Soldiers into Politicians*, 232.
15. Carbone, "Ten Years of Multiparty Politics"; De Zeeuw, *Political Party Development*; Manning, "Constructing Opposition"; Manning, *Making of Democrats*; Soderberg Kovacs, "When Rebels Change"; Manning, *Politics of Peace*.
16. Fortna and Huang, "Democratization after Civil War"; Zuercher et al., *Costly Democracy*.
17. Fortna and Huang, "Democratization after Civil War," 806.
18. Ishiyama, "Civil Wars and Party Systems."
19. We utilized the high estimates for battle deaths provided as they were more closely correlated with the best estimates provided (when available) than either the low estimate or an average between high and low estimates.
20. Lacina and Gleditsch, "Monitoring Trends in Global Combat."
21. Allison, "The Legacy of Violence"; Bueno de Mesquita, "Rebel Tactics"; Christia, *Alliance Formation in Civil Wars*; Fjelde and Nilsson, "Rebels Against Rebels"; Ishiyama and Batta, "Swords into Plowshares"; Mampilly, *Rebel Rulers*; Staniland, *Networks of Rebellion*; Weinstein, *Inside Rebellion*.
22. Doyle and Sambanis, *Making War and Building Peace*; Fortna, "Does Peacekeeping Keep Peace?"; Hartzell et al., "Stabilizing the Peace."
23. Altier et al., "Violence, Elections and Party Politics"; Brathwaite, "The Electoral Terrorist."
24. Ishiyama, "Civil Wars and Party Systems," 443.
25. The relationship between conflict intensity, measured here in terms of battle deaths, and the intensity of political cleavages could run in either direction. If deep cleavages predate conflict, it is unlikely to produce an effect different from what we'd see if conflict produced the cleavages. Either way, cleavages intensify.
26. Collier et al., "On the Duration of Civil War"; Hartzell et al., "Stabilizing the Peace"; Mason and Fett, "How Civil Wars End"; Regan, "Third-Party Interventions."
27. De Zeeuw, *Soldiers into Politicians*, 233.
28. Doyle and Sambanis, *Making War and Building Peace*.
29. Fortna and Huang, "Democratization after Civil War."
30. A conflict episode is a continuous period of active conflict years, with active conflict defined per UCDP-PRIO Armed Conflict dataset criteria. See Gleditsch et al., "Armed Conflict." An episode ends when it is followed by a year in which there are fewer than 25 battle-related deaths.
31. Note that there are multiple conflict episodes in most countries, multiple AOGs for some conflict episodes, and a number of armed groups that participate in more than one conflict episode. See Appendix 1 for a list of countries, conflict episodes, AOGs and parties.
32. Altier et al., "Violence, Elections and Political Parties"; Brathwaite, "The Electoral Terrorist"; Ishiyama and Batta, "Swords into Ploughshares."
33. We also later focus on the substantive impacts of each variable in our estimate. The estimates remain unchanged whether cluster robust standard errors are used or not, as clustering only alters the standard error and p-value used for measuring confidence. As we are interested in a more exploratory analysis in a relatively small dataset, we are less concerned about setting arbitrary thresholds of statistical significance.
34. This was done utilizing a stepwise algorithm to remove variables with a high variance inflation factor.
35. Fisher, *Statistical Methods*; Gelman and Stern, "The Difference between 'Significant' and 'Not Significant'"; Gill, "The Insignificance of Null Hypothesis."
36. Interpretation is based on the results from our second model.
37. Ishiyama, "Civil Wars and Party Systems," 445.

FROM BULLETS TO BALLOTS

38. Ishiyama and Batta, "Swords into Plowshares"; Manning, *Making of Democrats.*
39. Kalyvas, *Logic of Violence*; Weinstein, *Inside Rebellion.*
40. Manning and Berg, "Bilateral vs. Multilateral Peacebuilding."

Bibliography

Allison, Michael. "The Transition from Armed Opposition to Electoral Opposition in Central America." *Latin American Politics and Societies* 48 (2006): 137–162. doi:10.1353/lap.2006.0040

Allison, Michael. "The Legacy of Violence on Post-Civil War Elections: The Case of El Salvador." *Studies in Comparative International Development* 45 (2010): 104–124. doi:10.1007/s12116-009-9056-x

Altier, Mary Beth, Susanne Martin, and Leonard B. Weinberg. "Introduction to the Special Issue on Violence, Elections, and Party Politics." *Terrorism and Political Violence* 25, no. 1 (2013): 1–7. doi:10.1080/09546553.2013.733241

Bethany, Lacina, and Nils Petter, Gleditsch. "Monitoring Trends in Global Combat: A New Dataset of Battle Deaths." *European Journal of Population* 21 (2005): 145–166.

Brathewaite, Robert. "The Electoral Terrorist: Terror Groups and Democratic Participation." *Terrorism and Political Violence* 25, no. 1 (2013): 53–74. doi:10.1080/09546553.2013.733251

Bratton, Michael, and Nicholas van de Walle. *Democratic Experiments in Africa: Regime Transitions in Comparative Perspective.* Cambridge, UK: Cambridge University Press, 1997.

Bueno de Mesquita, Ethan. "Rebel Tactics." *Journal of Political Economy* 121, no. 2 (2013): 323–357. doi:10.1086/670137

Burnell, Peter. "Globalising party politics in emerging democracies." *Conference on Globalising Democracy - Party Politics in Emerging Democracies*, JUL, 2005, Univ Warwick, Warwick, UK, 2006.

Carbone, Giovanni. "Continuidade na Renovacao? Ten Years of Multiparty Politics in Mozambique: Roots, Evolution, and Stabilisation of the Frelimo-Renamo Party System." *The Journal of Modern African Studies* 43, no. 3 (2005): 417–442. doi:10.1017/S0022278X05001035

Christia, Fotini. *Alliance Formation in Civil Wars.* Cambridge, UK: Cambridge University Press, 2013.

Clapham, Christopher, ed. *African Guerillas.* Oxford: James Currey, 1998.

Collier, Paul, Anke Hoeffler, and Måns Söderbom. "On the Duration of Civil War." *Journal of Peace Research* 41 (2004): 253–273. doi:10.1177/0022343304043769

Curtis, Devon. "Transitional Governance in the Democratic Republic of Congo (DRC) and Burundi." In *Interim Governments: Institutional Bridges to Peace and Democracy?*, edited by Karen Guttieri and Jessica Piombo, 690. Washington, DC: United States Institute of Peace, 2007.

Curtis, Devon, and Jeroen de Zeeuw. "Rebel Movements and Political Party Development in Post-Conflict Societies: A Short Literature Review." Program on States and Security, Ralph Bunche Institute for International Studies, The Graduate Center at City University of New York, 2009. Accessed April 14, 2013. http://www.statesandsecurity.org/_pdfs/CurtisZeeuw.pdf.

De Zeeuw, Jeroen. *Soldiers into Politicians: Transforming Armed Opposition groups After Civil War.* Boulder: Lynne Rienner, 2007.

De Zeeuw, Jeroen. "Political Party Development in Post-War Societies: The Institutionalization of Parties and Party Systems in El Salvador and Cambodia." Ph.D. diss., University of Warwick, 2009.

Deonandan, K., D. Close, and G. Prevost, eds. *From Revolutionary Movements to Political Parties.* New York, NY: Palgrave MacMillan, 2007.

Doyle, Michael, and Nicolas Sambanis. *Making War and Building Peace: United Nations Peace Operations.* Princeton, NJ: Princeton University Press, 2006.

Dudouet, Veronique, Hans J. Giessmann, and Katrin Planta. *From Combatants to Peacebuilders: A Case for Inclusive, Participatory and Holistic Security Transitions.* Berlin: Berghof Foundation, 2012. www.berghof-foundation.org/fileadmin/redaktion/Publications/Papers/Policy_Reports/PolicyPaper_dudouetetal.pdf.

FROM BULLETS TO BALLOTS

Europa Online. *Europa Regional Surveys of the World*. Vols. 1–9. Multiple Years: 1990–2015.

Fisher, R. A. *Statistical Methods, Experimental Design, and Scientific Inference*. Oxford: Oxford University Press, 1990.

Flores, Thomas Edward, and Irfan Nooruddin. "The Effect of Elections on Postconflict Peace and Reconstruction." *The Journal of Politics* 74, no. 2 (2012): 558–570. doi:10.1017/S0022381611001733

Fortna, Virginia Paige. "Does Peacekeeping Keep Peace? International Intervention and the Duration of Peace after Civil War." *International Studies Quarterly* 48 (2004): 269–292. doi:10.1111/j.0020-8833.2004.00301.x

Fjelde, Hannah, and Desiree Nilsson. "Rebels Against Rebels: Explaining Violence Between Rebel Groups." *Journal of Conflict Resolution.* 56, no. 4 (2012): 604–628. doi:10.1177/0022002712439496

Fortna, Virginia Page, and Reyko Huang. "Democratization after Civil War: A Brush-Clearing Exercise." *International Studies Quarterly* 56 (2012): 801–808. doi:10.1111/j.1468-2478.2012.00730.x

Garibay, David. "De la lutte armée à la lutte électorale, itinéraires divergents d"un choix insolite, une comparaison à partir des cas centraméricains et colombien." *Revue Internationale de Politique Comparée* 12, no. 3 (2005): 283–297. doi:10.3917/ripc.123.0283

Gelman, Andrew, and Hal Stern. "The Difference Between "Significant" and "Not Significant" is not Itself Statistically Significant." *The American Statistician* 60, no. 4 (2006): 328–331. doi:10.1198/000313006X152649

Gill, Jeff. "The Insignificance of Null Hypothesis Significance Testing." *Political Research Quarterly* 52, no. 3 (1999): 647–674. doi:10.1177/106591299905200309

Gleditsch, Nils Petter, et al. "Armed Conflict 1946–2001: A New Dataset." *Journal of Peace Research* 39, no. 5 (2002): 615–637. doi:10.1177/0022343302039005007

Grzymala-Busse, Anna. *Redeeming the Communist Past.* Cambridge, UK: Cambridge University Press, 2002.

Harbom, Lotta, Stina Högbladh, and Peter Wallensteen. "Armed Conflict and Peace Agreements." *Journal of Peace Research* 43(2006): 617–631.

Harmel, R., and K. Janda. "An Integrated Theory of Party Goals and Party Change." *Journal of Theoretical Politics* 6 (1994): 259–287. doi:10.1177/0951692894006003001

Hartzell, Caroline, Matthew Hoddie, and Donald Rothchild. "Stabilizing the Peace after Civil War: An Investigation of Some Key Variables." *International Organization* 55 (2001): 183–208. doi:10.1162/002081801551450

Högbladh, Stina, 2011. "Peace agreements 1975–2011 - Updating the UCDP Peace Agreement dataset", In *2012, States in Armed Conflict 2011*, edited by Pettersson Thérése, and Lotta Themnér. Uppsala: Uppsala University, Department of Peace and Conflict Research Report 99.

Huang, Reyko. "The Wartime Origins of Postwar Democracy: Civil War, Rebel Governance, and Political Regimes." Ph.D. diss. , Columbia University, 2012.

Imai, Kosuke, Gary King, and Olivia Lau. "Toward A Common Framework for Statistical Analysis and Development." *Journal of Computational and Graphical Statistics* 17, no. 4 (2008): 892–913. doi:10.1198/106186008X384898

Ishiyama, J. "Civil Wars and Party Systems." *Social Science Quarterly* 95, no. 2 (2014): 425–447. doi:10.1111/ssqu.12020

Ishiyama, J. "Party Organization and the Political Success of the Communist Successor Parties." *Social Science Quarterly* 82 (2001): 844–864. doi:10.1111/0038-4941.00063

Ishiyama, J. "Communist Parties in Transition: Structures, Leaders and Processes of Democratization in Eastern Europe." *Comparative Politics* 27 (1995): 147–177. doi:10.2307/422162

Ishiyama, J. "The Sickle or the Rose?: Previous Regime Types and the Evolution of the Ex-Communist Parties in Post-Communist Politics." *Comparative Political Studies* 30 (1997): 299–330. doi:10.1177/0010414097030003002

Ishiyama, J. "The Communist Successor Parties and Party Organizational Development in Post-Communist Politics." *Political Research Quarterly* 52 (1999): 87–112. doi:10.1177/106591299905200104

Ishiyama, John, and Ana Batta. "Swords into plowshares: The organizational transformation of rebel groups into political parties." *Communist and Post-Communist Studies* 44 (2011): 369–379. doi:10.1016/j.postcomstud.2011.10.004

Jarstad, Anna K., and Timothy Sisk, eds. *From War to Democracy: Dilemmas of Peacebuilding.* Cambridge, UK: Cambridge University Press, 2008.

Kalyvas, Stathis N. *The Logic of Violence in Civil War*. Cambridge, UK: Cambridge University Press, 2006.

Kalyvas, Stathis N., and Laia Balcells. "International System and Technologies of Rebellion: How the End of the Cold War Shaped Internal Conflict." *American Political Science Review* 104 (2012): 415–429. doi:10.1017/S0003055410000286

Kitschelt, Herbert, et al. *Post-Communist Party Systems*. Cambridge, UK: Cambridge University Press, 1999.

Kreutz, Joakim. "How and When Armed Conflicts End: Introducing the UCDP Conflict Termination Dataset." *Journal of Peace Research* 47 (2010): 243–250. doi:10.1177/0022343309353108

Kumar, Krishna, and Jeroen de Zeeuw. "International Support for Political Parties in War-torn Societies." In *Political Parties in Conflict-prone Societies: Regulation, Engineering and Democratic Development*, edited by Benjamin Reilly and Per Nordlund, 261–285. Tokyo: United Nations University Press, 2008.

Lacina, Bethany, and Nils Petter Gleditsch. "Monitoring Trends in Global Combat: A New Dataset of Battle Deaths." *European Journal of Population / Revue européenne de Démographie* 21, no. 2–3 (2005): 145–166. doi:10.1007/s10680-005-6851-6

Lotta Themner, and Peter Wallensteen. "Armed Conflicts, 1946–2013." *Journal of Peace Research* 51 (2014): 541–554.

Mampilly, Zachariah Cherian. *Rebel Rulers: Insurgent Governance and Civilian Life during War*. Cornell, NY: Cornell University Press, 2011.

Manning, Carrie. "Constructing opposition in Mozambique: Renamo as political party." *Journal of Southern African Studies* 24, no. 1 (1998): 161–189. doi:10.1080/03057079808708571

Manning, Carrie. *The Politics of Peace in Mozambique: Post-Conflict Democratization, 1992–2000*. Westview: Praeger, 2002.

Manning, Carrie. "Armed Opposition Groups into Political Parties: Comparing Bosnia, Kosovo and Mozambique." *Studies in Comparative International Development* 39 (2004): 54–76. doi:10.1007/BF02686315

Manning, Carrie. "Party-Building on the Heels of War: El Salvador, Bosnia, Kosovo and Mozambique." *Democratization* 14 (2007): 253–272. doi:10.1080/13510340701245777

Manning, Carrie. *The Making of Democrats: Party-Building and Elections in Post Conflict Bosnia, El Salvador, and Mozambique*. New York, NY: Palgrave MacMillan, 2008.

Manning, Carrie, and Louis-Alexandre Berg. "Bilateral vs. Multilateral Peacebuilding in Africa." In *Africa in World Politics*, edited by John Harbeson and Donald Rothchild, 211–236. Boulder: Westview Press, 2013.

Mansfield, Edward D., and Jack Snyder. *Electing to Fight: Why Emerging Democracies Go to War*. Cambridge, MA: MIT Press, 2007.

Mason, T. David, and Patrick J. Fett. "How Civil Wars End: A Rational Choice Approach." *Journal of Conflict Resolution* 40 (1996): 546–568. doi:10.1177/0022002796040004002

Mattes, Michaela, and Burcu Savun. "Fostering Peace after Civil War: Commitment Problems and Agreement Design." *International Studies Quarterly* 53 (2009): 737–759. doi:10.1111/j.1468-2478.2009.00554.x

Nohlen, Dieter, ed. *Elections in the Americas: A Data Handbook. Vol. 1: North America, Central America, and the Caribbean*. Oxford: Oxford University Press, 2005.

Nohlen, Dieter, Florian Grotz, and Christof Hartmann, eds. *Elections in Asia and the Pacific: A Data Handbook*. Oxford: Oxford University Press, 2001.

Nohlen, Dieter, Michael Krennerich, and Berhard Thibaut, eds. *Elections in Africa: A Data Handbook*. Oxford: Oxford University Press, 1999.

Ogura, K. "Seeking State Power: The Communist Party of Nepal (Maoist)." *Berghof Series Resistance/Liberation Movements and Transitions to Politics* 3 (2011): 1–56.

Panebianco, Angelo. *Political Parties: Organization and Power*. Cambridge, UK: Cambridge University Press, 1988.

Paris, Roland. *At War's End: Building Peace after Civil Conflict*. Cambridge, UK: Cambridge University Press, 2004.

Pool, David. *From Guerillas to Government: The Eritrean People's Liberation Front*. Oxford: James Currey, 2001.

Porto, João Gomes, Chris Alden, and Imogen Parsons. *From Soldiers to Citizens: Demilitarization of Conflict and Society*. Aldershot: Ashgate, 2007.

FROM BULLETS TO BALLOTS

Putzel, James. "Do No Harm: International Support for Statebuilding." Paris: OECD DAC Fragile State Group, 2010.

Randall, Vicky, ed. *Political Parties in the Third World*. London: Sage Publications, 1988.

Regan, Patrick M. "Third-Party Interventions and the Duration of Intrastate Conflicts." *Journal of Conflict Resolution* 46 (2002): 55–73. doi:10.1177/0022002702046001004

Regan, Patrick M., and Aysegul Aydin. "Diplomacy and Other Forms of Intervention in Civil Wars." *Journal of Conflict Resolution* 50 (2006): 736–756. doi:10.1177/0022002706291579

Reilly, Benjamin. "Political Engineering and Party Politics in Conflict-Prone Societies." *Democratization* 13, no. 5 (2006): 811–827. doi:10.1080/13510340601010719

Reilly, Benjamin, and Per Nordlund, eds. *Political Parties in Conflict-prone Societies: Regulation, Engineering and Democratic Development*. Tokyo: United Nations University Press, 2008.

Sartori, Giovanni. *Parties and Party Systems: A Framework for Analysis*. Cambridge: European Consortium for Political Research Press, 2005.

Smith, Ian. "Where are They Now? Former Sole Legal Party Performance in Competitive Elections." Presented at the Annual Meeting of the Midwest Political Science Association, 2010.

Soderberg Kovacs, Mimmi. "When Rebels Change their Stripes: Armed Insurgents in Post-War Politics." In *From War to Democracy: Dilemmas of Peacebuilding*, edited by Anna K. Jarstad and Timothy Sisk, 105–133. Cambridge, UK: Cambridge University Press, 2008.

Staniland, Paul. *Networks of Rebellion: Explaining Insurgent Cohesion*. Cornell, NY: Cornell University Press, 2014.

United States Institute of Peace. "Peace Agreements Digital Collection." http://www.usip.org/category/publications/peace-agreements.

United States Institute of Peace. *Guiding Principles for Stabilization and Reconstruction*. Washington: U.S. Institute of Peace, 2009.

Uppsala Conflict Data Program. "UCDP Actor Dataset v. 2.1–2012." Accessed November 12, 2013. www.ucdp.uu.se, 2012.

Walter, Barbara. "Does Conflict Beget Conflict? Explaining Recurrent Civil War." *Journal of Peace Research* 41 (2004): 371–388. doi:10.1177/0022343304043775

Ward, Michael, Brian Greenhill, and Kristin Bakke. "The Perils of Policy by p-value: Predicting Civil Conflicts." *Journal of Peace Research* 47, no. 4 (2010): 363–375. doi:10.1177/0022343309356491

Weinstein, Jeremy. *Inside Rebellion: The Politics of Insurgent Violence*. Cambridge, UK: Cambridge University Press, 2006.

Wimpelmann, Torunn. "The Aid Agencies and the Fragile State Agenda." CMI Working Paper 21, 2006. Accessed June 29, 2012. http://bora.cmi.no/dspace/bitstream/10202/71/1/Working%20paper%20WP%202006-21.pdf.

Zuercher, Christoph, Carrie Manning, Kristie D. Evenson, Rachel Hayman, Sarah Riese, and Norah Roehner. *Costly Democracy: Peacebuilding and Democratization after Civil War*. Stanford: Stanford University Press, 2013.

Rebel-to-party transformations in civil war peace processes 1975–2011

Mimmi Söderberg Kovacs[†] and Sophia Hatz

Department of Peace and Conflict Research, Uppsala University, Uppsala, Sweden

ABSTRACT
Previous research has established the critical relevance of better understanding the conditions that either facilitate or obstruct rebel-to-party transformations for the sake of strengthening the prospects for both peace and democracy in post-war societies. In this study, we contribute to this growing research agenda in two ways. We first present and analyse data collected by the Uppsala Conflict Data Program (UCDP) on all peace agreements that contain specific rebel-to-party provisions during the time period 1975–2011. Second, we introduce new data on rebel-to-party outcomes during the same time period. The descriptive findings confirm several of our theoretical expectations. Rebel-to-party provisions are exclusive to the post-Cold War era, and are commonly included in peace agreements with third-party presence. Somewhat surprisingly, we have seen almost twice as many agreements with such provisions in Africa compared to other regions, and only in peace agreements in governmental conflicts. However, we find several cases of rebel-to-party outcomes in territorial conflicts. Our data also confirm that rebel-to-party provisions are neither necessary nor sufficient for rebel-to-party outcomes, and highlight the potential relevance of other political provisions also supporting the group's political integration.

Introduction

In 2012, Colombia's oldest and largest guerilla movement, known as FARC (Revolutionary Armed Forces of Colombia), initiated peace talks with the Colombian government in Havana, Cuba. As part of the negotiations, it was eventually publicly announced that the warring parties had agreed on the terms for the political participation of the guerrilla group in democratic politics, a landmark agreement generally considered to constitute one of the key pillars of a comprehensive peace deal in the Colombian conflict.[1] The deal signals the willingness of the parties to consider an end to the armed struggle in exchange for political participation. One option would be to transform the disarmed military movement into a legal political party. If so, they would not be the first rebel group to venture down this path.

[†]The authors have contributed to this article in different ways. Söderberg Kovacs is the principal author of the article and had the main responsibility for definitions and coding decisions, the coding of rebel-to-party outcomes, and the interpretation of results. Hatz had the main responsibility for the construction of the dataset and accumulation of results, including all tables and figures.

FROM BULLETS TO BALLOTS

The transformation of formerly armed non-state actors to political parties within the context of civil war peace processes has grown to become a relatively frequent phenomenon in the last couple of decades. From having opposed, rejected or being excluded from participation and representation, former rebel groups have contested democratic elections, and sometimes gain political prominence and influence in post-war decision-making institutions. The rationale expressed by domestic and international peace-makers for supporting such processes of integration have commonly centred on the need to increase the perceived benefits of peace over war, and to encourage the strengthening of a multi-party political system.[2] Beyond such pragmatic considerations, there may also be more deep-seated attempts to try to eradicate or address some of the underlying grievances that contributed to the outbreak of the civil war in the first place.

This trend has generated a small but quickly growing research agenda that has generated increased knowledge of the causes, dynamics and outcome of rebel-to-party transformations in civil war peace processes.[3] Other studies have looked more closely at the potential effects of rebel-to-party transformation on the process of democratization.[4] Yet, in spite of the increasing attention to this topic, we do not yet know enough about the overall trends and patterns associated with rebel-to-party transformations. Such knowledge is imperative if we are to understand more about both the causes and consequences of these processes. This study thus speaks to this overarching research question: Under what conditions are rebel groups that sign peace agreements more likely to subsequently transform into political parties?

We contribute to answer this question by systematically mapping out and assessing the frequency and scope of the inclusion of rebel-to-party provisions in peace agreements in civil-war peace processes during the time period 1975–2011, as well as the frequency and scope of completed rebel-to-party transformations by rebel signatories during the same time period. We first present and analyse data collected by the Uppsala Conflict Data Program (UCDP) on all peace agreements that contain specific rebel-to-party provisions during the time period 1975–2011. Second, we present new data on rebel-to-party outcomes during the same time period. We take a closer look at all non-state armed actors who were signatories to peace agreements during this period (some of which included explicit rebel-to-party provisions), and establish whether they become political parties or not in the post-settlement period.

The descriptive findings confirm several of our theoretical expectations. Rebel-to-party provisions are exclusive to the post-Cold War era, and are commonly included in peace agreements with third party presence. Somewhat surprisingly, we have seen almost twice as many agreements with such provisions in Africa compared to other regions, and only in peace agreements in governmental conflicts. However, we find several cases of rebel-to-party outcomes in territorial conflicts. Our data also confirm that rebel-to-party provisions may encourage rebel-to-party outcomes but are neither necessary nor sufficient for such processes to take place, and that rebels who transform into political parties often sign agreements containing several political provisions supporting the group's political integration.

Previous research on rebel-to-party transformations

Following in the footsteps of the increase in negotiated peace settlements in the 1990s, a soon burgeoning literature emerged which attempted to identify the conditions under which armed groups sign peace agreements and when these peace deals are likely to hold and prove durable.[5] Within this strand of research, a couple of studies identify the transformation of the former warring parties into peaceful political contenders as a critical element of the conflict resolution process in civil wars.[6]

With the point of departure in this literature, a few studies have looked more closely at the conditions under which rebel-to-party transformation are sometimes are carried out and completed and sometimes not.[7] For example, Söderberg Kovacs finds that rebel groups are more likely to become viable political parties when the leadership of the group is united on the decision to abandon the armed struggle and enter peaceful politics, when the rebel group has a relatively high level of popular support among the domestic population, and when key international actors and donors recognize the rebel group as a legitimate political actor.[8] Manning has carried out pioneering work in this strand of research, explicitly linking the post-war fate of rebel parties to the group's ability to generate resources and support in a changing political context.[9] Manning was also among the first to point to the relevance of both intra-party factors and the constraints and opportunities posed by the external political environment. Dodouet and colleagues have made important contributions to the debate by brining light on the viewpoints of the groups themselves.[10] Grisham asks what factors are critical in determining the spectrum of choices available to armed groups when they transform from one type of organization to another, ranging from political parties, criminal organizations to so-called terrorist organizations.[11] Hensell and Gerdes also consider several options for political integration, looking at the conditions under which former rebels emerge as part of the post-war political elite.[12]

A related yet separate strand of research in this field emanates primarily from the field of security studies, where researchers have attempted to better understand the dynamics of hybrid politico-military organizations that engage in a dual military and political struggle within the framework of an unresolved armed conflict in an electoral democracy.[13] Notable cases include Hamas in the Palestinian territories, Hezbollah in Lebanon and the Provisional Irish Republican Army (PIRA)/Sinn Féin in Northern Ireland. This set of literature is relevant in that it discusses the conditions under which such groups create, sustain and develop political wings.

Another set of literature primarily takes its point of departure in the democratization and political party literature. Deonandan, Close and Prevost examine the extent to which former guerrilla movements that have become political parties have been able to continue to pursue a revolutionary agenda in an electoral context.[14] Söderberg Kovacs discusses the potential effects of rebel-to-party organizations on the prospects for democratic governance in post-war societies.[15] Allison finds that the character and performance of these armed groups during the war and their post-war electoral success are causally linked, pointing at their degree of popular support and group size as determining factors.[16] In an in-depth case study of El Salvador, Allison establishes empirical support for the relationship between an armed group's wartime behaviour towards the civilian population in a particular area and post-war electoral support in the same locality.[17] Ishiyama and Marshall have contributed to our understanding of the rationale behind candidate recruitment by former rebel parties and whom they select to run as their electoral frontmen.[18] Ishiyama and Batta argue that former rebel parties are more likely than other parties to experience internal political schisms over the identity and structure of the new party once they enter normal politics.[19] Research has also recently emerged on the role played by so called warlord democrats – individuals linked to the armed struggle who enter politics – and the implications for post-war security.[20]

The majority of empirical contributions to this scholarly debate have been studies of single cases of rebel-to-party transformations.[21] There has also been a range of works comparing a small number of cases within the same region or across regions.[22] However, so far there have been no attempts to systematically collect data on a larger set of cases, and look at patterns and trends when it comes to rebel-to-party transformations across both time and space. In particular, we lack information about the extent to which peace agreements signed in internal armed conflicts contain explicit provisions for the transformation of the warring parties to legal political parties, and the frequency and scope of completed rebel-to-party transformations following the ending of civil wars through negotiated settlements.

Theoretical expectations

Rebel-to-party provisions in peace agreements

When should we expect to see peace agreements with rebel-to-party provisions? It was not until after the end of the Cold War and the onset of the so-called liberal peacebuilding era, that the (re)introduction or strengthening of democracy in post-war societies came to be considered as an integral part of the peace-building process.[23] According to Matanock, there were no provisions regarding the holding of elections in peace agreements prior to 1990, confirming that this year represents an important watershed in term of the strategy and approach to conflict resolution.[24] Hence, this suggests that *we should see more rebel-to party provisions in peace agreements signed in the post-Cold War era (H1).*

Following the same logic, *we should also expect rebel-to-party provisions to be more common in peace negotiations including third-party actors (H2).* Case studies of rebel-to-party transformations show that the involved third-party actors sometimes suggest the inclusion of rebel-to-party provisions based on their experience from other peace processes. However, the primary parties may ultimately be the ones who argue for their inclusion at the negotiation table. For example, the idea of transforming the Revolutionary United Front (RUF) in Sierra Leone into a political party was first presented to the politically inexperienced armed movement by representatives of the international community during the Abidjan peace process in 1996. Everyone in the RUF delegation, however, welcomed the idea, and such provisions were later replicated in the Lomé accords in 1999.[25]

Should we be more likely to see the inclusion of rebel-to-party provisions in peace agreements in some civil war settings compared to others? There is little to suggest that this should be the case. From the case study literature, we know rebel-to-party transformations have occurred across various geographical regions and in different types of armed conflicts, ranging from the Free Aceh Movement (GAM) in Indonesia, to the Kosovo Liberation Army (KLA) in Kosovo, and to the National Council for the Defense of Democracy – Forces for the Defense of Democracy (CNDD-FDD) in Burundi.[26] Some of these rebel groups fought in territorial conflicts, and others in conflicts over government power. Hence, *there is no reason to expect the frequency of rebel-to party provisions to vary across regions (H3a) or types of civil wars (H3b).*

Should we expect rebel-to-party provisions to occur more frequently in some types of peace agreement compared to others? Based on some of the most well-documented case studies, notably Renamo in Mozambique and the Farabundo Martí National Liberation Front (FMLN) in El Salvador, it is reasonable to expect such provisions to be more common in peace agreements that aim to end a civil war by addressing the entire armed conflict and the full range of incompatibilities at stake, rather than including them as a stand-alone feature in a so-called partial peace accord that addresses only a limited aspect of the conflict in question.[27] Likewise, we should expect rebel-to-party provisions to be more common in comprehensive peace agreements signed between all warring parties to the conflict, rather than part of a separate peace deal between one non-state armed group and the government in question. Hence, *rebel-to-party provisions should be more common in full (H4a) and comprehensive (H4b) peace agreements*.

Rebel-to-party outcomes following peace agreements

When should we expect to see rebel-to-party outcomes? Based on findings from previous research, *we should see more rebel groups transform into political parties following the signing of peace agreements in the post-Cold War era (H5)*. Although the third wave of democratization expanded the global sphere of democratic countries significantly, the number of electoral democracies boomed after the end of the Cold War.[28] As the early 1990s also saw a peak in the ending of a large number of prolonged civil wars with their dynamics intrinsically tied to the Cold War logic, we can expect the number of rebel-to-party transformations to also increase from around this time. However, *there is no reason to expect rebel-to-party outcomes to vary across various geographical regions (H6a) or conflict settings (H6b)*.

To what extent does the content of the peace agreement matter in this respect? Theoretically, *we should be more likely to see former rebel groups become political parties following peace agreements that contain rebel-to-party provisions (H7)*. De Zeeuw argues that the formal recognition in the peace agreement of a rebel movement's right to transition into a legitimate political organization offers the group "a strong impetus for change".[29] Case studies also point to the importance of explicit guarantees provided by the text of the peace agreement.[30] Such provisions should have the potential to ensure the establishment of some kinds of legal and political pre-conditions in the post-agreement period. They could also be seen as an indicator of the willingness of the rebel group to attempt such a process at the time of the signing of the accord.

The chances of successful *rebel-to-party transformations should also increase if the rebel group has signed peace agreements containing other political provisions that also aim at supporting the group's political integration in the post-war period (H8)*. Rebel-to-party provisions are likely to function as one mechanism among many that serve as a guarantee for the political and organizational survival of the rebel group after its disarmament and demobilization. According to De Zeeuw, the holding of post-war elections and power-sharing mechanisms influence the room for manoeuvre in the post-war political space and hence increase the incentives for the rebel group to become a political party.[31]

Lastly, *we should also expect more rebel-to-party outcomes following peace agreements with third party involvement (H9)*. Söderberg Kovacs has established the importance of international legitimacy and support in rebel-to-party transformations.[32] De Zeeuw and van de Goor likewise point to the critical relevance of the international community in supporting rebel-to-party transformations, ranging from assistance for DDR programmes, political training courses, logistical support, political and diplomatic pressure and financial assistance.[33] Manning has documented the considerable impact played by third party actors involved in the Mozambique peace process in supporting Renamo's transition to peaceful politics.[34]

The rebel-to-party dataset

The Rebel-to-Party Dataset includes all organized, armed, non-state actors who have signed peace agreements with governments between 1975 and 2011 based on the UCDP Peace Agreement Dataset. Only agreements signed by at least two opposing warring parties in that armed conflict and agreements that address a stated incompatibility over government, territory, or both, are included.[35] In the Peace Agreement Dataset, peace agreements are coded as "dyadic" if at least one of the warring parties to the conflict is excluded from the agreement and "comprehensive" if all are included. They are considered "full" if the warring parties agree to settle the whole incompatibility as opposed to a "partial", when only part of the incompatibility is addressed, and "peace process agreements" when "one or more dyads agree to initiate a process that aims to settle the incompatibility".[36] Of the 216 peace agreements included in the Peace Agreement Dataset, 196 were peace agreements aimed at solving intra-state conflicts or civil wars. The subsequent analysis only includes these agreements and the 93 non-state armed groups that have signed at least one such agreement. The Peace Agreement Dataset also provides information about the provisions in the text of each accord, including whether it contained specific rebel-to-party provisions and other political provisions, and whether there were third party mediators or signatories.[37] Each of these non-state armed signatories is also identified as a unique actor in the UCDP Actor Dataset, from which we are able to draw on additional information about the group.[38]

The added unique contribution of the Rebel-to-Party Dataset is to provide information regarding rebel-to-party outcomes. This proved a challenging task, as no such information was readily available. We first attempted to match the 93 rebel group names with lists of political parties in the World Bank Political Institutions Dataset and the CLEA Political Parties Dataset. However, this process could only identify rebel groups that were or became political parties using the same name when they entered politics. It also raised doubts about the causal process involved beyond the mere correlation of names. All rebel groups were therefore manually coded on a case-by-case basis. The primary source used was the conflict descriptions in the UCDP Conflict Encyclopedia.[39] Additional and complementary information was sought in country reports from the Freedom House and the International Crisis Group, CIA World Fact Book country summaries and in reports on elections from the International Foundations for Electoral Systems (IFES) Election Guide, and the African Democracy Encyclopaedia from the Electoral Institute for Sustainable Democracy in Africa (EISA). Occasionally, more specific country sources were also consulted, such as political party websites, news sites and academic journals and books. Based on these sources, brief case descriptions were written for each country, including the coding decision. This material was subsequently circulated among country experts. Based on their feedback, both conflict descriptions and coding decisions were updated accordingly.

What is a rebel-to-party transformation? As noted above, for the definition of "rebel group", we rely on the definition developed by the UCDP, where an "opposition organization" in a state-based armed conflict is defined as "any non-governmental formally organized group of people having announced a name for their group and using armed force to influence the outcome of the stated incompatibility".[40] For the definition of "political party", we rely on classical works in the field of political science, where we learn that the aim of a political party is to win public office and attain political power, and that the electoral process is the means to achieve this aim.[41] The focus on elections is critical, because it differentiates political parties from other organizations with similar goals.[42] However, what is left out in these definitions is a discussion about other means to achieve these political ends, such as violence. For the purpose of our study, however, such a distinction is essential. Thus, in this study a political party is an organization that seeks to attain power primarily through non-violent means in electoral competition with one or more similar organizations within the political system. What follows is that the essence of the transformation from a rebel group into a political party lies both in the change of *means* of the political struggle, from arms to votes, and the *arena* of that struggle, inside or outside the legal framework of politics. Hence, the rebel group must both abandon the armed struggle and continue the political struggle through active participation within the political system in order to be considered to have transformed into a political party.

When applying these definitions to our cases, however, and trying to systematically code rebel-to-party transformations, one is undoubtedly confronted with empirical grey zones. For example, armed groups may sign peace agreements and become political parties and participate in electoral competition while still continuing to pursue the armed struggle, such as for example Fatah in the Palestinian territories. In this study, such cases are not considered cases of rebel-to-party transformations. As noted by Berti, the dual engagement of hybrid politico-military organizations should not per definition be interpreted as a step towards further moderation, as the group may only participate in electoral politics to increase its strength and solidify its position in the armed struggle.[43] In addition, during a civil war, many armed groups are often linked, directly or indirectly, openly or covertly, to functioning non-violent political parties.[44] A case in point is the relationship between the Provisional IRA and Sinn Féin during the armed conflict in Northern Ireland. Although Sinn Fein continued to function as the political voice of the republican movement after the war, the PIRA did not transform into a political party after it had disarmed and disbanded. Hence, for our purposes, this is not considered a rebel-to-party transformation. A third and final challenging coding criterion concerns the lower threshold for when we may usefully call a formerly armed group a functioning political party. It was decided that as long as an identifiable and significant part of the formerly armed group establishes a political party that registers a party name, selects candidates and participates in elections (national or local), it is considered a rebel-to-party transformation.

Descriptive findings

Rebel-to-party provisions in peace agreements

How many peace agreements contain provisions that allow the formerly armed group to transform into political parties? Of the 196 peace agreements included in the UCDP

FROM BULLETS TO BALLOTS

Peace Agreement Dataset, 30 (15.3%) included explicit rebel-to-party provisions in the text of the agreement. These agreements are listed in Table 1, along with the names of the rebel groups, sorted by country and year the agreement was signed.

As noted, some countries – notably Burundi and Chad – are overrepresented, with several peace agreements that contain such provisions. The proportion of conflicts

Table 1. Intrastate peace agreements with rebel-to-party provisions, 1991–2011.

Country	Peace agreement	Year	Rebel group(s)
Angola	The Bicesse Agreement	1991	UNITA
Burundi	Arusha Peace and Reconciliation Agreement for Burundi	2000	Palipehutu; CNDD; Frolina
Burundi	Ceasefire Agreement between the Transitional Government of Burundi and the Conseil National pour la Défense de la Démocratie–Forces pour la Défense de la Démocratie (CNDD-FDD)	2002	Palipehutu/FNL
Burundi	The Pretoria Protocol on Outstanding Political, Defence and Security Power Sharing in Burundi	2003	CNDD-FDD
Burundi	The Global Ceasefire agreement between Transitional Government and the CNDD-FDD of Mr. Nkrunziza	2003	CNDD-FDD
Burundi	The Pretoria Protocol on Political, Defence and Security Power Sharing in Burundi	2003	CNDD-FDD
Burundi	Agreement of Principles Towards Lasting Peace, Security and Stability	2006	Palipehutu/FNL
Burundi	Declaration of the Summit of the Heads of State and Government of the Great Lakes region on the Burundi Peace Process	2008	Palipehutu/FNL
Cambodia (Kampuchea)	Agreement on a Comprehensive Political Settlement of the Cambodia Conflict "The Paris Agreement"	1991	KR; KPNLF; FUNCINPEC
Chad	El Geneina agreement	1992	FNT
Chad	Tripoli 1 Agreement	1993	CNR
Chad	Bangui-2 Agreement	1994	CSNPD
Chad	National reconciliation agreement	1997	FNT
Chad	Donya agreement	1998	FARF
Chad	Yebibou agreement 2005	2005	MDJT
Colombia	Acuerdo final Gobierno Nacional-Ejército Popular De Liberación	1991	EPL
Congo, Democratic Republic of (Zaire)	23 March 2009 Agreement	2009	CNDP
Djibouti	Accord de paix et de la reconciliation nationale	1994	FRUD
Djibouti	Accord de reforme et concorde civile	2001	FRUD/AD
El Salvador	The Chapultepec Peace Agreement	1992	FMLN
Guatemala	The Agreement on the Basis for the Legal Integration of the URNG	1996	URNG
Mozambique	Agreement on Establishment and Recognition of Political Parties	1991	Renamo
Mozambique	The Acordo Geral de Paz (AGP)	1992	Renamo
Rwanda	Arusha Accords	1993	FPR
Sierra Leone	Abidjan Peace Agreement	1996	RUF
Sierra Leone	Lom Peace Agreement	1999	RUF
Sierra Leone	Abuja Ceasefire Agreement	2000	RUF
Sudan	Addis Ababa Agreement	2011	SPLM/A/North
Tajikistan	Agreement between the President of the Republic of Tajikistan, E.S. Rakhmonov, and the leader of the United Tajik Opposition, S.A. Huri, on the results of the meeting held in Moscow 23 December 1996	1996	UTO
Tajikistan	The Moscow Declaration – General agreement on the Establishment of Peace and National Accord in Tajikistan	1997	UTO

Total number of intrastate peace agreements with rebel-to-party provisions: 30. Source: UCDP Peace Agreement Dataset, v2.0 2012.

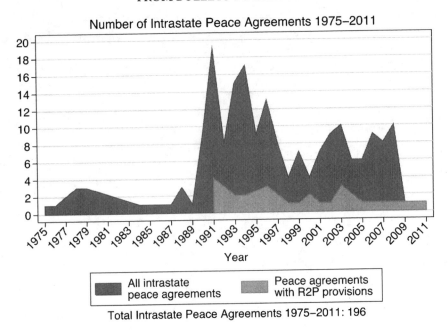

Figure 1. Number of intrastate peace agreements with and without rebel-to-party provisions (1975–2011).

where such provisions have been part of a negotiated settlement is therefore lower than the numbers first appear to suggest. Several rebel groups have also signed more than one agreement with rebel-to-party provisions. What is the overall trend regarding the inclusion of rebel-to-party provisions across time and space in peace agreements? Figure 1 illustrates changes over time in annual number of peace agreements and peace agreements with rebel-to-party provisions, from 1975 through 2011.

As expected, there were no peace agreements with rebel-to-party provisions before 1991 (H1). Such agreements are thus exclusively a product of the post-Cold War era. The year 1991 was also the peak for such provisions, with four peace agreements including rebel-to-party provisions that year: the Bicesse agreement in Angola, the Paris peace agreement in Cambodia, the accord between the government and the Popular Liberation Army (EPL) in Colombia, and one of the peace process agreements leading to the general peace agreement in Mozambique. When it comes to the distribution of rebel-to-party provisions across space, however, the findings are not in line with the theoretical expectations (H2a). Figure 2 shows the number of peace agreements with and without rebel-to-party provisions by region for the Post-Cold War period 1991–2011.

As shown in Figure 2, the largest share of all peace agreements during this time period were signed in Africa (104 of 172, or 60.5%). This is also where we find the greatest share of peace agreements containing rebel-to-party provisions (24 of 104 peace agreements in Africa, or 23.1%). Hence, more than one-fifth of all peace agreements signed in Africa in the post-Cold War period contained rebel-to-party provisions. As noted previously, however, some African countries are overrepresented here, with several such agreements. Some rebels groups have also signed more than one such agreement. In contrast, the share of agreements containing rebel-to-party provisions

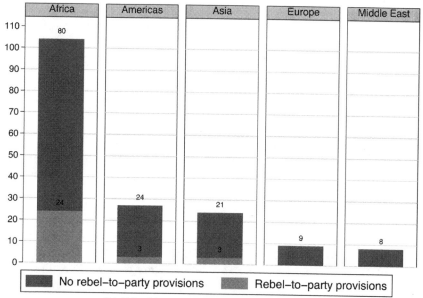

Figure 2. Number of intrastate peace agreements with and without rebel-to-party provisions, by region (1991–2011).

is much smaller in both Americas and Asia, with three out of 27 agreements (11%) and three out of 24 agreements (12.5%), respectively. There were also no rebel-to-party provisions in peace agreements in either the Middle East or Europe during this time period. The frequency of rebel-to-party provisions in peace agreements also varies across different types of civil wars (H2b). As shown in Table 2 below, explicit rebel-to-party provisions have only been included in agreements addressing conflicts over government power, and not in any of the 40 agreements signed in conflicts over territory.

As shown in Table 3, and according to our expectations, the overwhelming majority of peace agreements with rebel-to-party provisions (27 of 30 cases or 90%) have third-party involvement, in the form of mediators or signatories to the agreements (H3). Contrary to our expectations, however, there are a few more dyadic agreements compared to comprehensive agreements that contain rebel-to-party provisions (H4a). In line with H4b, there are a few more full agreements compared to partial agreements or peace process agreements that contain rebel-to-party provisions, but the differences are negligible.

Table 2. Conflict incompatibility and rebel-to-party provisions (1975–2011).

	Without rebel-to-party provisions	With rebel-to-party provisions	Total
Territorial incompatibility	40 (24.1%)	0 (0.0%)	40 (20.4%)
Government incompatibility	126 (75.9%)	30 (100.0%)	156 (79.6%)
Total number intrastate peace agreements	166	30	196

Source: UCDP Peace Agreement Dataset, v2.0 2012.

FROM BULLETS TO BALLOTS

Table 3. Characteristics of intrastate peace agreements with rebel-to-party provisions (1975–2011).

	Count	Per cent
Comprehensive	13	43.3%
Dyadic	17	56.7%
Full	17	56.7%
Partial	11	36.7%
Peace process	2	6.7%
Third-party involvement	27	90.0%
Peace agreement ended	9	30.0%
Total intrastate peace agreements with RtP Provisions	30	100%

Source: UCDP Peace Agreement Dataset, v2.0 2012.

Rebel-to-party transformations following peace agreements

One of the key purposes of the Rebel-to-Party Dataset is to establish whether these non-state armed signatories to peace agreements subsequently emerged as political parties in the post-settlement period or not. As noted above, there are 93 groups included in the Rebel-to-Party Dataset. In total, 33 (35.5%) of these groups are considered to have completed rebel-to-party transformations according to our criteria. These groups are listed in Table 4, along with their names as political parties (the last known name of the party is stated) and the year of the last (most recent) peace agreement signed by the group. If this agreement included rebel-to-party provisions, this is indicated in the "Year" column (*).

Hence, almost one-third of all non-state signatories subsequently continue to pursue their goals within the legal political framework. This confirms that rebel-to-party transformations are not marginal or exceptional phenomena. Because our data are limited to signatory groups in negotiated settlements, which constitute only about one-third of all civil war endings, we only capture a small number of the total population of potential rebel-to-party transformations. Notably, non-signatory rebels turned political parties, such as the Revolutionary Front for an Independent East Timor (FRETILIN), and former rebels turned parties after military victories, such as the Ethiopian People's Revolutionary Democratic Front (EPRDF), are excluded. Many of the liberation movements that came to power after the end of colonial rule are also excluded, such as the People's Movement for the Liberation of Angola (MPLA) in Angola (which also falls outside the time period).

In line with our theoretical expectations, our descriptive data show that the great majority of the rebel-to-party transformations are post-Cold War cases (H5). The only exceptions to this trend are the two liberation movements in Zimbabwe who both transformed to political parties (and later merged to become the Zimbabwe African National Union – Patriotic Front, ZANU-PF) after the Lancaster House agreement in 1979. The South West Africa People's Organization (SWAPO) in Namibia signed a peace agreement with South Africa for its independence in 1978, but elections were not held until November 1989, in which the former liberation movement secured the majority of the votes in the Assembly.[45]

As expected, rebel-to-party transformations occur across various geographical regions and conflict settings (H6a and H6b). In absolute numbers, the greatest share of rebel-to-party transformations is found in Africa (19 of 33 or 57.6%). However, Africa also had by far the largest amount of non-state armed signatories during this time period with a total of 58 rebel groups, with only 19 (32.7%) of these transforming

FROM BULLETS TO BALLOTS

Table 4. Rebel-to-party transformations following intrastate peace agreements (1975–2011).

Country	Rebel group name	Year	Political party name
Afghanistan	Islamic Society of Afghanistan	1996	Jamiat-e Islami Afghanistan (Salahud-din Rabbani)
Afghanistan	Unity Party	1993	Hezbe-Wahdat-e Islami (Khalili)
Angola	National Union for the Total Independence of Angola	2002	National Union for the Total Independence of Angola
Bangladesh	People's Solidarity Association/Peace Force	1997	Chittagong Hill Tracts United People's Party
Bosnia-Herzegovina	Croatian Republic of Bosnia-Herzegovina	1994	Croatian Democratic Union of BiH
Bosnia-Herzegovina	Serbian Republic of Bosnia-Herzegovina	1995	Serb Democratic Party
Burundi	National Council for the Defense of Democracy	2000*	National Council for the Defense of Democracy
Burundi	National Council for the Defense of Democracy/Forces for the Defense of Democracy	2003*	National Council for the Defense of Democracy/Forces for the Defense of Democracy
Burundi	National Liberation Front	2000*	Frolina
Burundi	Party for the Liberation of the Hutu People	2000*	Palipehutu
Burundi	Party for the Liberation of the Hutu People/Forces for National Liberation	2008*	National Forces of Liberation
Cambodia (Kampuchea)	Khmer People's National Liberation Front	1991*	Buddist Liberal Democratic Party
Cambodia (Kampuchea)	United National Front for an Independent, Neutral, Peaceful and Cooperative Cambodia	1991*	United National Front for an Independent, Neutral, Peaceful and Cooperative Cambodia
Colombia	People's Liberation Army	1991*	Esperanza, Paz y Libertad
Congo, Democratic Republic of (Zaire)	Congolese Rally for Democracy	2003	Congolese Rally for Democracy
Congo, Democratic Republic of (Zaire)	Movement for the Liberation of Congo	2003	Movement for the Liberation of Congo
Djibouti	Front for the Restoration of Unity and Democracy	1994*	Front pour la Restauration de l'Unité Democratique
El Salvador	Farabundo Marti Front for National Liberation	1992*	Farabundo Marti Front for National Liberation
Guatemala	Guatemalan National Revolutionary Unity	1996*	Guatemalan National Revolutionary Unity
India	Tripura National Volunteers	1988	Indigenous Peoples Front of Tripura/ Indigenous Nationalist Party of Tripura
Indonesia	Free Aceh Movement	2005	Partai Aceh
Liberia	National Patriotic Front of Liberia	1996	National Patriotic Party
Mozambique	Mozambican National Resistance	1992*	Mozambique National Resistance
Nepal	Communist Party of Nepal/Maoist	2006	Unified Communist Party of Nepal (Maoist)
Rwanda	Rwandan Patriotic Front	1993*	Rwandan Patriotic Front
Sierra Leone	Revolutionary United Front	2000*	Revolutionary United Front-Party
South Africa	African National Congress	1993	African National Congress
South Africa	South West Africa People's Organization	1978	South West Africa People's Organization
Sudan	Sudanese People's Liberation Movement/Army	2005	Sudanese People's Liberation Movement
Uganda	National Resistance Army	1985	National Resistance Movement
Yugoslavia	Kosovo Liberation Army	1999	Yugoslavia Democratic Party of Kosovo
Zimbabwe (Rhodesia)	Patriotic Front	1979	Zimbabwe African National Union-Patriotic Front

(Continued)

33

FROM BULLETS TO BALLOTS

Table 4. Continued.

Country	Rebel group name	Year	Political party name
Zimbabwe (Rhodesia)	Zimbabwe African People's Union	1975	Zimbabwe African People's Union

Primary sources: UCDP Peace Agreement Dataset (2012), UCDP Actor Dataset (2012) and UCDP Conflict Encyclopedia (2013). Additional sources are detailed in the codebook. Observations: 33. Groups shown are those which have signed intrastate peace agreements between 1975 and 2011 and are also political parties. If the last (most recent) peace agreement signed by the rebel included rebel-to-party provisions, this is indicated in the column "Year" with a star*.

into political parties. This is to be compared to both Asia and Americas, where about half of the rebel signatories became political parties, with eight out of 15 signatories (53.3%) and three out of six signatories (50%), respectively. Three out of 12 signatories (25%) transformed into political parties in Europe. The only region with no rebel-to-party transformations was the Middle East, but it only had two rebel signatories in total during the time period. Hence, the spread of rebel-to-party outcomes is a relatively fair reflection of the geographical distribution of the total population of non-state armed signatories. In line with our expectation, there have been rebel-to-party outcomes following both territorial and governmental conflicts. We find seven cases (constituting about one-fourth of all rebel-to-party transformation) of non-state armed groups in territorial conflicts that become political parties, such as for example the Serb Democrat Party (SDS) in Bosnia Herzegovina.

Our data also confirm that non-state armed actors that sign agreements with specific rebel-to-party provisions appear overrepresented among those that become political parties compared to other signatories (H7). Almost half (45.5%) of the rebel groups who later transformed into political parties signed at least one peace agreement that included rebel-to-party provisions. But in the total population of rebel-to-party transformations more than half (54.5%) did not sign an agreement with such provisions. Hence, this confirms that the inclusion of rebel-to-party provisions is far from a necessary or sufficient factor for such processes to take place.

As shown in Table 5, and in line with our expectations, former rebels becoming political parties have more often than other groups signed peace agreements containing other political provisions aiming at supporting the group's political integration in the post-war period (H8). For example, 78.8% in our total population of 33 cases of rebel-to-party transformations signed at least one agreement that also included provisions for the holding of elections. This is in contrast to our total population of signatory rebel groups, where only 40% did so. In addition, about half of them have signed at least one agreement that included explicit wording about some form of power-sharing

Table 5. Characteristics of peace agreements and rebel-to-party outcomes (1991–2011).

Signed at least one agreement with:	Rebel groups	RtP groups	All
Rebel-to-party provisions	16.7%	45.5%	26.9%
Provisions for elections	40.0%	78.8%	53.8%
Provisions for integration in interim government	28.3%	54.5%	37.6%
Provisions for integration in government	26.7%	36.4%	30.1%
Provisions for integration in civil service	16.7%	6.1%	12.9%
Provisions for power-sharing in government	18.3%	42.4%	26.9%
Third party involvement	86.7%	87.9%	87.1%
Total number of rebel groups	60	33	93

Source: UCDP Peace Agreement Dataset, v2.0 2012; RtP Dataset.

mechanisms ("integration in interim government", "integration in government" or "power sharing"), which is also more than in the total population of rebel signatories. Contrary to our expectations, however, rebel-to-party groups do not seem to be different from other signatories when it comes to having signed peace agreements with a third party presence (H9). The presence of third parties is equally high for all peace agreements during this period.

Discussion

The descriptive findings presented above regarding the frequency and scope of both rebel-to-party provisions in peace agreements and rebel-to-party outcomes empirically confirm many claims and assumptions in the previous literature on rebel-to-party transformations. They also shed new light on some aspects and issues, and raise further questions about the explanatory factors and causal mechanisms involved, something that lay beyond the scope of this study. Further research is needed, in terms of both large-N studies making use of the Rebel-to-Party Dataset in combination with other systematic data available for rebel groups, and in-depth small-N studies that seek to carve out the more detailed workings of these processes. Below we highlight some potential areas for future research based on the findings emerging from this study.

First, there are still a number of unanswered questions regarding why rebel-to-party provisions are included in peace agreements in the first place. While we are able to show that the great majority of such agreements involve third parties, this is also true for most peace agreements during this time period. What is the more specific role of third parties in this respect, and what are the potential learning effects from one peace process to another? In-depth case studies and interviews with third-party actors may provide important insights into this question. Another set of potentially relevant explanatory variables relate to the character and background of the armed groups concerned. Are certain types of non-state armed group more inclined than others to push for, or agree to, such settlement provisions? Our data may throw some light on this issue. For example, in the category of armed groups who did not sign agreements with specific rebel-to-party provisions yet later emerged as political parties, we find many groups who became the dominant political party in the post-war period. This includes, for example, groups like the ANC in South Africa, SWAPO in Namibia, and the National Patriotic Front of Liberia (NPFL) in Liberia. In these cases, it is reasonable to assume that the group was rather confident about gaining political influence, or even winning, in the post-war elections and had little need to include provisions that guaranteed their political survival. Some of these groups also had functioning and well-organized political organizations already prior to or during the war. This is in stark contrast to cases such as Renamo in Mozambique and the RUF in Sierra Leone, where the rebel groups were more dependent on the inclusion of such provision in the peace agreement and often referred to the rights granted to them by the peace accord in this respect, not least for soliciting financial support during the implementation period.[46] Our finding that we have only seen rebel-to-party provisions in governmental conflicts may also hold some clues to answering this question. Rebel groups in such conflicts are much more likely to be concerned about securing access to political power within the existing political system, while rebel groups in territorial conflicts are primarily concerned with securing political space through some form of arrangement for self-determination.

Second, while we are able to show that rebel groups who later emerge as political parties have more frequently than other rebel groups signed agreements with specific rebel-to-party provisions, our findings also indicate the importance of other explanatory factors at work which deserve further investigation. For example, we are able to demonstrate that rebels who subsequently emerged as political parties often sign peace agreements with several political provisions aiming at securing their post-war political integration. Detailed case studies may provide more information about the different considerations and trade-offs that rebel groups make in this respect. It is, for example, possible that under certain condition provisions for electoral participation or power-sharing may function as an equally effective means of securing political survival for non-state armed groups. As argued by Matanock, non-state armed actors frequently opt for provisions for participatory post-war elections in peace accords because the holding of such elections attracts significant international attention and engagement, which in turn put pressure on the government party to uphold its part of the peace deal by increasing the costs of non-compliance.[47] Following this logic, rebel groups may have a greater chance of securing their post-war political survival by opting for elections rather than rebel-to-party provisions. Another cluster of explanatory factors worth exploring more systematically relates to the degree of violence and insecurity in the post-settlement period. For example, we know that in the case of the National Congress for the Defence of the People (CNDP) in the Democratic Republic of Congo (DRC), the group signed a peace agreement on 23 March 2009 which granted the armed group the right to become a legal political party. However, the failure to implement the agreement led to renewed violence in eastern DRC in 2012 and the emergence of the M23 rebellion.[48] Lastly, we need more detailed systematic data about the specific support – diplomatic, financial, training – that third parties provide to rebel groups during the transition in order to be able to draw any conclusions about the relative impact of such support across a large set of cases.

Conclusions

As noted by De Zeeuw, transforming a rebel movement into a political party is "arguably one of the hardest peace-building challenges" and case studies have shown that such processes are often complex, time-consuming, and have a high risk of failure. [49] A growing research agenda has therefore emerged which attempts to better understand the causes, dynamics and outcome of rebel-to-party transformations. From having been an issue of marginal consideration in the periphery of traditional research fields, the topic is gradually gaining attention in its own right. In this article, we have attempted to contribute to this emerging debate in two different ways: first, by proving empirical support for the frequency and scope of rebel-to-party provisions in peace agreements in the time period 1975–2011; second, by collecting and presenting novel data on rebel-to-party transformations following peace settlements in civil wars, for the same time period. The results point to some interesting findings with implications for both ongoing research on these issues and policy-making and practice in this field.

Building on data collected by the UCDP, we are able to show that about every sixth peace agreement during the time period under study contained explicit rebel-to-party provisions. We were also able to demonstrate that such provisions are a novelty of the post-Cold War era, that they have been more commonly included in peace agreements in Africa and in peace deals with a third-party presence. Our data also show that

FROM BULLETS TO BALLOTS

they have only been included in peace agreements in governmental conflicts, and that they have been somewhat more frequent in dyadic and full peace agreements. On rebel-to-party outcomes, our data showed that out of a total of 93 non-state signatories in civil war settlements, almost one-third subsequently emerged as a political party. The great majority of such transformations occurred after the end of the Cold War, but, unlike rebel-to-party provisions, rebel-to-party transformations have occurred across various regions and following both governmental and territorial conflicts. Such transformations appear somewhat more likely following the signing of agreements with rebel-to-party provisions, but we also highlight the potential relevance of other political provisions supporting the group's post-war political integration.

Notes

1. "Colombia agrees Farc political participation", BBC News, 6 November 2013. http://www.bbc.com/news/world-latin-america-24842432.
2. Curtis and De Zeeuw, Rebel Movements.
3. E.g., De Zeeuw, "Understanding Political Transformations"; Manning, "Party-Building"; Söderberg Kovacs, Rebels to Statesmen.
4. E.g., Deonandan, Close, and Prevost, Movements to Parties; Ishiyama and Batta, "Swords into Plowshares."
5. E.g., Darby and MacGinty, Management of Peace; Darby and MacGinty, Contemporary Peacemaking; Hampson, Nurturing Peace; Hartzell, "Explaining Stability"; Licklider, Stopping the Killing; Nilsson, Shadow of Settlement; Svensson, Elusive Peacemakers; Walter, Committing to Peace; Zartman, Elusive Peace.
6. E.g., Lyons, Demilitarizing Politics; Stedman, "Policy Implications."
7. E.g., De Zeeuw, Soldiers to Politicians; Söderberg Kovacs, Rebels to Statesmen.
8. Söderberg Kovacs, Rebels to Statesmen.
9. Manning, "Armed Opposition Groups"; Manning, "Party-Building."
10. Dudouet, War to Politics.
11. Grisham, Transforming Violent Movements.
12. Hensell and Gerdes, "Exit from War."
13. E.g., Berti, Armed Political Organizations; Van Engeland and Rudolph, Terrorism to Politics; Weinberg, Pedahzur, and Perliger, Parties and Terrorist Groups.
14. Deonandan, Close, and Prevost, Movements to Parties.
15. Söderberg Kovacs, Rebels to Statesmen.
16. Allison, "Transition from Armed."
17. Allison, "The Legacy of Violence."
18. Ishiyama and Marshall, "Candidate Recruitment."
19. Ishiyama and Batta, "Swords into Plowshares."
20. Themnér, Warlord Democrats.
21. E.g., Aguswandi and Zunzer, Successful Transition; Hachhethu, "Communist Party Nepal"; Klapdor, Rebels to Politicians; Manning, Politics of Peace; Mitton, "Engaging Disengagement"; Stange and Patock, "Rebels to Rulers."
22. E.g., De Zeeuw, Soldiers to Politicians; Grisham, Transforming Violent Movements; Manning, "Party-Building"; Söderberg Kovacs, Rebels to Statesmen.
23. Jarstad and Sisk, War to Democracy.
24. Matanock, "International Insurance."
25. Bangura and Söderberg Kovacs, "Shape Shifters."
26. E.g., Bekaj, KLA and Kosovo; Nindorera, "Transformation of CNDD-FDD"; Ogura, Seeking State Power.
27. Álvarez, War to Democratic; Manning, Politics of Peace; Manning, "RENAMO'S Electoral Success"; Wade, "Success of FMLN."
28. Huntington, The Third Wave.
29. De Zeeuw, Soldiers to Politicians, 19.
30. Söderberg Kovacs, Rebels to Statesmen.

31. De Zeeuw, *Soldiers to Politicians*, 19–20.
32. Söderberg Kovacs, Rebels to Statesmen.
33. Zeeuw and van de Goor, "International Involvement", 239.
34. Manning, Politics of Peace.
35. UCDP, *Peace Agreement Dataset*, v.2.1.
36. Ibid.,10.
37. Ibid., 6.
38. UCDP, v.2.1 *Actor Dataset*.
39. UCDP Conflict Encyclopedia.
40. UCDP, Definitions.
41. Sartori, *Parties and Systems*, 64; Downs, *Economic Theory Democracy*, 25; Duverger, *Political Parties*, xxiii.
42. Panebianco, *Political Parties*, 6.
43. Berti, *Armed Political Organizations*, 4–8.
44. Mehler, "Rebels and Parties."
45. Melber, *Understanding Namibia*.
46. Söderberg Kovacs, Rebels to Statesmen.
47. Matanock, "International Insurance."
48. International Crisis Group, "Eastern Congo."
49. De Zeeuw, *Soldiers to Politicians*, 1.

Acknowledgements

We would like to thank Isak Svensson at the Department of Peace and Conflict Research, Uppsala University, as well as two anonymous reviewers and the Editor of this Special Issue for many useful suggestions. We also gratefully acknowledge financial support from Riksbankens Jubileumsfond: The Swedish Foundation for Humanities and Social Sciences.

Disclosure statement

No potential conflict of interest was reported by the authors.

Bibliography

Aguswandi, and Wolfram Zunzer. *The Successful Transition of the Garakan Acheh Merdeka (Free Aceh Movement, GAM): From Politics to Arms to Politics Again*. Transition Series, Resistance/Liberation Movements and Transitions to Politics. Berlin: Berghof Center, 2012.
Allison, Michael. "The Transition from Armed Opposition to Electoral Opposition in Central America." *Latin American Politics and Society* 48 (2006): 137–162. doi:10.1353/lap.2006.0040
Allison, Michael. "The Legacy of Violence on Post-civil War Elections: The Case of El Salvador." *Studies in Comparative International Development* 45 (2010): 104–124. doi:10.1007/s12116-009-9056-x
Álvarez, Alberto Martín. *From Revolutionary War to Democratic Revolution: The Farabundo Martí National Liberation Front (FMLN) in El Salvador*. Transition Series, Resistance/Liberation Movements and Transitions to Politics. Berlin: Berghof Center, 2010.
Bekaj, Armend R. *The KLA and the Kosovo War: From Intra-State Conflict to Independent Country*. Transition Series, Resistance/Liberation Movements and Transitions to Politics. Berlin: Berghof Center, 2010.

FROM BULLETS TO BALLOTS

Bangura, Ibrahim, and Mimmi Söderberg Kovacs. "Shape Shifters in the Struggle for Survival: Post-war Politics in Sierra Leone." In *Warlord Democrats in Africa: The Security Effects of Integrating Ex-Military Leaders into Electoral Politics*, edited by Anders Themnér. London: Zed Publishing, forthcoming 2016.

Berti, Benedetta. *Armed Political Organizations: From Conflict to Integration*. Baltimore: The Johns Hopkins University Press, 2013.

Curtis, Devon, and Jeroen De Zeeuw. *Rebel Movements and Political Party Development in Post-Conflict Societies: A Short Literature Review*. New York: Ralph Bunche Institute for International Studies, 2010.

Darby, John, and Roger MacGinty, eds. *The Management of Peace Processes*. London: Macmillan Press Ltd, 2000.

Darby, John, and Roger MacGinty, eds. *Contemporary Peacemaking: Conflict, Violence and Peace Processes*. Houndmills: Palgrave Macmillan Ltd, 2003.

Deonandan, Kalowatie, David Close, and Gary Prevost, eds. *From Revolutionary Movements to Political Parties: Cases from Latin America and Africa*. New York: Palgrave Macmillan, 2007.

De Zeeuw, Jeroen, ed. *From Soldiers to Politicians: The Transformation of Rebel Movements After War*. Boulder: Lynne Rienner Publishers, 2008.

De Zeeuw, Jeroen. "Understanding the Political Transformation of Rebel Movements." In *From Soldiers to Politicians: Transforming Rebel Movements after War*, edited by Jeroen De Zeeuw. Boulder: Lynne Rienner Publishers, 2008.

Dudouet, Veronique. *From War to Politics: Resistance/Liberation Movements in Transition*. Berlin: Berghof Research Center, 2009.

Duverger, Maurice. *Political Parties: Their Organization and Activity in the Modern State*. 2nd ed. London: Methuen & Co. Ltd., 1959.

Downs, Anthony. *An Economic Theory of Democracy*. New York: Harper & Row Publishers, 1957.

Grisham, Kevin E. *Transforming Violent Political Movements: Rebels today, what tomorrow?* London: Routledge, 2014.

Hachhethu, Krishna. "The Communist Party of Nepal (Maoist): The Transformation from an Insurgency Group to a Competitive Political Party." *European Bulletin of Himalayan Research* 33–34 (2008–2009): 39–71.

Hampson, Fen O. *Nurturing Peace: Why Peace Settlements Succeed or Fail*. Washington, D.C. United States Institute of Peace Press, 1996.

Hartzell, Caroline A. "Explaining the Stability of Negotiated Settlements to Intrastate Wars." *Journal of Conflict Resolution* 43, no. 1 (1999): 3–22. doi:10.1177/0022002799043001001

Hensell, Stephan, and Felix Gerdes. "Exit from War: The Transformation of Rebels into Post-war Political Elites." Paper presented at the 7th ECPR General Conference in Bordeaux 4–7 September, 2013.

Huntington, Samuel P. *The Third Wave: Democratization in the Late Twentieth Century*. Norman: University of Oklahoma Press, 1991.

International Crisis Group (ICG). Eastern Congo: Why Stabilisation Failed. Africa Briefing No. 91. Kinshasa/Nairobi/Brussels: International Crisis Group, 2012.

Ishiyama, Johan, and Anna Batta. "Swords into Plowshares: The Organizational Transformation of Rebel Groups into Political Parties." *Communist and Post-Communist Studies* 44 (2011): 369–379.

Ishiyama, John, and Michael Marshall. "Candidate Recruitment and Former Rebel Parties." *Party Politics* 21, no. 3 (2015): 591–602. doi:10.1177/1354068813487125

Jarstad, Anna K., and Timothy Sisk. *From War to Democracy: Dilemmas of Peacebuilding*. Cambridge: Cambridge University Press, 2008.

Klapdor, Dominik. *From Rebels to Politicians: Explaining Rebel-to-Party Transformations after Civil War. The Case of Nepal*. Working Paper Series No. 09–94, Development Studies Institute, London School of Economics, 2009.

Licklider, Roy, ed. *Stopping the Killing: How Civil Wars End*. New York: New York University Press, 1993.

Lyons, Terrence. *Demilitarizing Politics: Elections on the Uncertain Road to Peace*. Boulder: Lynne Rienner Publishers, 2005.

Manning, Carrie L. *The Politics of Peace in Mozambique: Post-Conflict Democratisation, 1992–2000*. Westport: Praeger, 2002.

Manning, Carrie. "Armed Opposition Groups into Political Parties: Comparing Bosnia, Kosovo, and Mozambique." *Studies in Comparative International Development* 39, no. 1 (2004): 54–76.

Manning, Carrie. "Party-building on the Heels of War: El Salvador, Bosnia, Kosovo and Mozambique." *Democratization* 14, no. 2 (2007): 253-272. doi:10.1080/13510340701245777

Manning, Carrie. "RENAMO's Electoral Success." In *From Soldiers to Politicians. Transforming Rebel Movements after War*, edited by Jeroen De Zeeuw. Boulder: Lynne Rienner Publishers, 2008.

Matanock, Aila M. "International Insurance: Explaining Provisions for Participatory Post-Conflict Elections in Peace Agreement Design." Unpublished paper for book manuscript, University of California, Berkeley: Berkeley, C.A, 2014.

Mehler, Andreas. "Rebels and parties. The impact of armed insurgency on representation in the Central African Republic." *Journal of Modern African Studies* 49, no. 1 (2011): 115-139.

Melber, Henning. *Understanding Namibia: The Trial of Independence*. London: Hurst Publishers, 2014.

Mitton, Kiernan. "Engaging Disengagement: The Political Reintegration of Sierra Leone's Revolutionary United Front." *Conflict, Security and Development* 8, no. 2 (2008): 193-222.

Nilsson, Desirée. In the Shadow of Settlement: Multiple Rebel Groups and Precarious Peace. Ph.D. dissertation, Department of Peace and Conflict Research, Uppsala University, 2006.

Nindorera, Willy. "Burundi: The Deficient Transformation of the CNDD-FDD." In *From Soldiers to Politicians: Transforming Rebel Movements after War*, edited by Jeroen De Zeeuw. Boulder: Lynne Rienner Publishers, 2008.

Ogura, Kiyoko. *Seeking State Power: The Communist Party of Nepal (Maoist)*. Transition Series, Resistance/Liberation Movements and Transitions to Politics. Berlin: Berghof Center, 2008.

Panebianco, Angelo. *Political Parties: Organization and Power*. Cambridge: Cambridge University Press, 1989.

Richards, Paul. "Sierra Leone: The Marginalization of the RUF." In *From Soldiers to Politicians: Transforming Rebel Movements after War*, edited by Jeroen De Zeeuw. Boulder: Lynne Rienner Publishers, 2008.

Sartori, Giovanni. *Parties and Party Systems: A Framework for Analysis*. Vol. 1. Cambridge: Cambridge University Press, 1976.

Stange, Gunnar, and Roman Patock. "From Rebels to Rulers and Legislators: The Political Transformation of the Free Aceh Movement (GAM) in Indonesia." *Journal of Current Southeast Asian Affairs* 29, no. 1 (2010): 95-120.

Stedman, Stephen John. "Policy Implications." In *Ending Civil Wars: The Implementation of Peace Agreements*, edited by S. J. Stedman, D. Rothchild, and E. M. Cousens. Boulder: Lynne Rienner Publishers, 2002.

Svensson, Isak. Elusive Peacemakers: A Bargaining Perspective on Mediation in Internal Armed Conflicts. Ph.D. dissertation, Department of Peace and Conflict Research, Uppsala University, 2006.

Söderberg Kovacs, Mimmi. From Rebels to Statesmen: The Transformation of Rebel Groups to Political Parties in Civil War Peace Processes. PhD dissertation, Uppsala University, 2007.

Söderberg Kovacs, Mimmi. "When Rebels Change Their Stripes: Armed Insurgents in Post-War Politics." In *From War to Democracy: Dilemmas of Peacebuilding*, edited by A. Jarstad and T. D. Sisk. Cambridge: Cambridge University Press, 2008.

Themnér, Anders, ed. *Warlord Democrats in Africa: The Security Effects of Integrating Ex-Military Leaders into Electoral Politics*. London: Zed Publishing, forthcoming 2016.

Van de Goor, Luc, and Jeroen De Zeeuw. "International Involvement in Rebel-to-Party Transformations." In *From Soldiers to Politicians: Transforming Rebel Movements after War*, edited by Jeroen De Zeeuw. Boulder: Lynne Rienner Publishers, 2008.

Van Engeland, Anisseh, and Rachel M. Rudolph. *From Terrorism to Politics*. Aldershot: Ashgate, 2008.

Wade, Christine. "El Salvador: The Electoral Success of the FMLN." In *From Soldiers to Politicians: Transforming Rebel Movements after War*, edited by Jeroen De Zeeuw. Boulder: Lynne Rienner Publishers, 2008.

Walter, Barbara F. *Committing to Peace: The Successful Settlement of Civil Wars*. Princeton: Princeton University Press, 2002.

Weinberg, Leonard B., Ami Pedahzur, and Arie Perliger. *Political Parties and Terrorist Groups*. London: Routledge, 2008.

Zartman, William I., ed. *Elusive Peace: Negotiating an End to Civil Wars*. Washington, D.C.: The Brookings Institution, 1995.

Does political inclusion of rebel parties promote peace after civil conflict?

Michael Christopher Marshall[a] and John Ishiyama[b]

[a]Department of Political Science, Miami University, Oxford, USA;
[b]Department of Political Science, University of North Texas, Denton, USA

ABSTRACT

Does the inclusion of rebel parties into the post-conflict political process help contribute to peace after the end of conflict? In this article we examine whether the transformation of rebel groups into political parties actually leads to the development of a durable peace after a civil war. Examining the likelihood of recurrence of civil wars in a country and recurrence of conflict in government–rebel group dyads after a settlement, we find that the inclusion and participation of former rebel parties in national government has an important impact on the likelihood of a durable post-settlement peace. Most importantly, *not* excluding major rebel parties from access to governing institutions is the most important factor in promoting post-conflict peace.

Does the inclusion of rebel parties into the post-conflict political process help contribute to a durable peace after the end of a conflict? In this article we examine whether the transformation of armed groups into political parties and their participation in the post-war political process actually leads to a durable peace following negotiated settlements. Recently there have been a number of studies that examine the process by which former rebel organizations "transform" after the end of a conflict. Much of this work is based on the assumption that understanding such transformations is important because inclusion of these former rebel parties into the political process will *actually lead to peace duration after civil wars*. Rather than examine this assumption, the literature has tended to focus either on whether former rebel groups decide to adapt to, evade, or exit the post-war political arena[1] or the organizational transformation of the rebel organization,[2] the candidate recruitment of former rebel parties[3] or on the electoral performance of such parties.[4] This article directly addresses the question of whether the long-term inclusion of rebel parties in the political process leads to a durable peace.

There is a long-held notion that inclusion of rebel groups in the peace process and the subsequent post-conflict political process will lead to a sustainable peace.[5] Some have argued that the transformation of rebel groups into political parties provides channels for both interest articulation and political process engagement for former rebels, thus incentivizing these groups to remain peaceful and adhere to the terms of a settlement.[6] Although several other scholars suggest that an inclusive peace settlement will also promote peace once peace has been secured, the evidence on this is rather mixed.[7]

However, most of the existing literature is limited to examining the impact of "short-term inclusion" into the peace process.[8] Short-term inclusion essentially involves including the former warring groups into a *negotiation process* that seeks to end a civil war. Some have argued that the likelihood for sustainable peace results from having an increased number of combatants included in the negotiation process, although there is considerable debate as to whether more or fewer groups better maintain peace.[9]

What is largely ignored, as Suazo points out, is what he terms "long-term inclusion", which focuses on "ensuring actors in a peace process have their interests heard after the process has been closed".[10] This involves the inclusion of former rebel parties in the process of governance *after* the peace process concludes, which involves winning electoral office and governing. Thus for the purposes of this article, *long-term inclusion* is defined as whether the former rebel parties participate in the political process and the process of governing (as opposed to being simply invited to the negotiation table). This does not necessarily refer to a period of time, only that the former rebel parties are included in governing beyond the settlement negotiation process. This definition also suggests that inclusion over a longer period of time (meaning over a number of elections) will lead to a longer lasting peace.

Although these processes are often connected, with short-term participation in the negotiation process leading to the former rebel groups attaining positions of power, this is not always the case. In many cases, peace settlements do not result in guaranteed positions for the rebels, only the promise of the introduction of elections (such as the settlements that ended the civil wars in Nepal, El Salvador, and Tajikistan). Further, short-term inclusion in the negotiation process does not mean that the rebel parties will continue in positions of governmental power over the longer term – many disappear or are systematically excluded – as was the case of the Islamic Renaissance Party in Tajikistan.

Empirically, however, what little literature there is that examines the long-term inclusion of rebel parties into the political process is limited to the investigation of a few select case studies. In this article we examine whether long-term inclusion of rebel parties into the political process (for example, participation via representation in government and access to the executive) promotes peace duration in post-civil war societies.[11] Using data from several post-conflict election sources, we examine whether former armed groups' inclusion into governance actually makes it more or less likely that a durable peace emerges.

Inclusion and peace duration

Although much attention has been paid to the development of former rebel parties, there is relatively little work on whether the inclusion of such parties into the political process actually contributes to peace. While some literature suggests that democracy may also result from inclusion, in this article we focus on whether inclusion fosters peace (a point which has been frequently suggested in the literature).

Much of the existing literature on inclusion focuses on the inclusion of rebel groups in the negotiations that lead to a peace settlement.[12] A prominent argument made in the literature is that post-conflict peace becomes more durable when all parties to a conflict are included in the negotiation process leading to a settlement.[13] For instance, Roy Licklider contends that in order to promote peace duration "every effort to bring all of the important players into the process" must be made "as soon as possible".[14] Ohlson and Söderberg suggest that an inclusive agreement is the best solution for a sustainable peace.[15]

There are two reasons why inclusion, at least in the "short run", should help promote peace duration. First, when parties to the conflict are excluded, this increases the risk that "spoilers" will emerge who may disrupt the agreement that is reached.[16] Hampson further argues that it is essential to include all the warring parties in the discussion concerning the post-war political order. This is because "If parties are excluded from these negotiations, or if their interests are not represented at the bargaining table, they will have a much stronger incentive to defect from the peace process and resort to violence to achieve their aims".[17] This is also evidenced in much of the literature on settlement and peace duration. As Nilsson points out, much of the literature in support of inclusion "suggests that if an actor on the outside continues to pursue the military course, this can have a destabilizing effect on the actors that have signed on to an agreement".[18]

The second reason is that inclusion allows for the parties involved in the conflict to gain greater representation in governing institutions. Hartzell argues that there is a credible commitment problem that exists between warring parties. These security concerns can be best addressed with the creation of power sharing institutions (for example, inclusive institutions).[19] Power sharing institutions foster "a sense of security among former enemies and encourage conditions conducive to a self-enforcing peace".[20] Overall, based upon this presumption, power sharing has become a common solution by scholars and policymakers designing institutions in post-conflict states.[21] In societies emerging out of a civil war, especially in ethnically divided societies, there is a trend towards designing political institutions that emphasize inclusiveness and participation in the government which is thought to promote trust and peace among warring parties.[22] This suggests that, in the long run, representation of rebel parties in government should lead to greater peace duration. However, this literature has focused mainly on the design of inclusive institutions, and not on whether inclusion after a civil war or civil conflict has actually happened.

Although attention has been paid to the effect of including former rebel groups in the short term on peace duration after the end of a civil wars, there is much less attention paid to the impact of long-term inclusion. There are some important exceptions. One such exception is the work of Suazo. He argues, based upon three case studies (El Salvador, Mozambique and Angola), that long-term inclusion (again defined as inclusion into the process of governance) has a positive effect on a sustainable peace. However, inclusion in the political process alone is not enough. Although the transformation of rebel groups into political parties "prove useful in allowing legal access and use of a country's political institutions as a way to further the group's political goals"[23] they are not "sufficient to ensure that a former rebel group will fully renounce the option of war as a channel toward power attainment".[24] Long-term inclusion that ensures that the rebel group achieves power provides an incentive to abide by the rules: "If a rebel group turned political party perceives that a given electoral performance is tied to a veritable chance to forward its political projects, it will start to regard the system as a legitimate power-procurement tool".[25] Thus, it is not only the opportunity to participate in elections, but gaining access to power for the former rebel groups that is the key to a sustainable peace in the long run.

Thus, the above literature suggests that the long-term inclusion of former rebel groups into the political process should lead to longer peace duration. However, what is meant by "peace" and "inclusion"? Although there has been some consensus in the literature on "peace" there has been less conceptual clarity on what is meant by "inclusion". Generally, peace duration in post-conflict countries has been defined very simply as the lack of a recurrence of war.[26] Based upon this, however, the literature on civil war recurrence has addressed peace in two ways.

First, there is the conception of "peace" as applying to individual dyads, involving government and former rebels groups. Much of this literature counts a "peace spell" (or period where war is absent) when a conflict between government and rebel group ends and continues until a conflict resumes between the pair of antagonists.[27] In this literature, peace is defined as less than 25 deaths per calendar year.[28] Thus, we define in operational terms a dyadic conflict as ended when a settlement has occurred between the government and a rebel group and produced at least six months of peace (where battle deaths in the dyad do not exceed 25). A restart of the conflict is the first year where at least 25 battle deaths are recorded in the dyad, thus ending the peace spell.

However, it is very likely that there may be multiple dyadic conflicts within a single country: when one is at peace, another may be in conflict. Indeed, for many scholars, the important question regarding peace is not whether there is the recurrence of conflict between the state and a rebel group, but whether peace is maintained within a country as a whole.[29] Therefore, in terms of an operational definition of peace in a country we use the definition of Mason et al.[30] For country level peace, we define a conflict as ended when peace settlement has produced at least six months of peace (where battle deaths have not exceeded 500 battle deaths). The restart of civil war is the first year that conflict causes at least 500 battle deaths.

Regarding our primary explanatory variables, political inclusion is defined as inclusion into either the legislature or the executive (the principal policy making and policy implementation institutions). We do not include the judiciary because, unlike other political institutions, the judiciary, generally, is not the primary policy making or policy implementing body. For the legislature we conceive of inclusion as involving the proportion of seats in the entire legislature (including upper and lower houses) held by the rebel groups. For the dyadic level, this would involve representation of a particular rebel group as a party in a given year.

For the national level this involves two types of legislative representation. The first is the total proportion of seats held by all former rebel groups in a given year. However, as much of the literature on "spoilers" has suggested, exclusion of one or more groups from the political process can lead to a higher likelihood of conflict resumption.[31] Thus, a second way to think of legislative inclusion at the national level is to measure whether one or more significant rebel groups are excluded from the process of governing.

Inclusion into the executive is also a key factor that may dampen the likelihood of conflict resumption. Johanna Birnir has suggested that an effective way to reduce the likelihood of conflict resumption in ethnic civil wars is to provide access to the executive.[32] This is because, in most developing countries, it is the executive, and particularly the ministerial portfolios in cabinet, that provides access to patronage resources and which count most politically. Thus, inclusion of former rebel groups should lead to a lowered likelihood of conflict resumption.

The above suggests the following three hypotheses. Hypotheses 1 and 3 refer to both national level and dyadic level civil conflicts. Hypotheses 1 and 2 refers only to national level civil war recurrence.

Hypothesis 1: For both national and dyadic levels, the greater the degree to which former rebel parties gain legislative representation, the less likely the recurrence of civil war and conflict.
Hypothesis 1a: When one or more former rebel groups are excluded from legislative representation, this should lead to a greater likelihood of national level civil war.
Hypothesis 2: For both national and dyadic levels, access to executive power will reduce the likelihood of civil war recurrence and conflict.

Design and methodology

To test the above hypotheses, we first constructed a data set based on all identified negotiated settlements from the Uppsala-PRIO Armed Conflict Data Project (otherwise known as UCDP).[33] The scope of this study is limited to negotiated settlements that led to at least one election following the end of the civil war from 1979 to 2014. We do not consider civil wars that end in either the victory of the government or the rebels, nor do we include where conflicts did not end in a settlement (such as a never ending cease fire). This is because we are interested in whether a long-term inclusion into the political process promotes peace, and long-term inclusion presupposes a settlement between government and rebels (which would not be the case if one side won or if the civil war never officially ended). The UCDP Peace Agreement Data identifies 69 settlements meeting our criteria. Thus, to test for national level peace duration we examine the duration of peace after 69 settlements in 46 different countries. For the second part of the analysis, which examines peace in dyads, we examine 118 dyads in 46 countries for the same period.[34] For the dependent variable we code whether in the country or in the dyad a war resumed in a given year. Table 1 reports the summary descriptive statistics for the data set.

Consistent with the existing literature, we define a peace after a settlement as beginning if, after six months, a civil war in a country (for example, exceeding 500 battle deaths) or a civil conflict in a dyad (for example, exceeding 25 battle deaths) has not occurred. At the national level, civil war resumption ("failure term") is defined as occurring in the first year where battle deaths in a country have exceeded 500. A dyadic conflict resumption is coded as a "1" in the first year a conflict has exceeded 25 battle deaths. The recurrence of civil war is coded as a "1" for the year a civil war recurred in a country and a civil conflict recurred in a dyad. Years where peace was maintained following a negotiated settlement were coded as a "0".

The primary independent variables for our study relate to *inclusion*. As mentioned above, inclusion involves both legislative and executive aspects, for example, whether the former rebel group attains access to representation in the legislature and access to the political executive (either via a cabinet portfolio or as chief executive).[35]

The first measure of inclusion is simply the natural log of the percent of legislative seats held by all former rebel groups. This can involve either one or multiple parties holding seats. We take the natural log of this variable because there are many former rebel parties that

Table 1. Descriptive statistics.

	National Level			Dyadic Level		
	MEAN	RANGE		MEAN	RANGE	
Dep. Variable						
Peace Duration In Years	7.566	1	33	7.952	1	34
Ind. Variables						
Logged %Seats	−2.203	−6.329	0.686	−3.124	−6.329	0
Major Party Excluded	0.357	0	1			
Executive Inclusion	0.577	0	1	0.432	0	1
UN Peacekeeping	0.596	0	1	0.591	0	1
Prop. Representation	0.729	0	1	0.759	0	1
Ethnic Fractionalization (ranges from 0 to 1, higher is more fractionalized)	0.578	0.130	0.950	0.581	0.130	0.950
Infant Mortality Rate (per 1000 live births)	4.082	2.219	5.003	4.021	1.435	5.029
Logged Oil and gas production by country (percent of exports)	1.388	0	3.324	1.446	0	3.324
Logged Battle Deaths (in thousands	8.923	4.025	11.885	8.968	3.296	11.886
Logged War Duration (Months)	4.281	2.485	6.356	4.385	2.484	6.597
Identity War	0.449	0	1	0.502	0	1
	N = 69 Settlements			N = 118 Dyads		

hold relatively few seats (or a distinct right skew in the distribution).[36] The second is a measure of whether one or more former rebel parties are excluded from representation in the legislature. We measure this as a simple dummy variable, where "1" is where at least one former rebel party was excluded from representation in the legislature, and where "0" indicated that all former rebel parties gained legislative representation.

We also include a dichotomous measure of former rebel party membership in a governing coalition, which is particularly important in understanding whether these parties are involved in the executive. Inclusion in the governing coalition status is measured as a binary variable, where "1" is equal to holding of the chief executive or ministerial portfolio and "0" is equal to exclusion of a former rebel party from the governing coalition. These measures of participation in post-conflict politics were collected using election data from PARLINE, the African Election Database, and information from *Political Parties of the World*.[37]

Beyond these primary explanatory variables that are used to test the hypotheses stated above, we also include a number of control variables. These include factors that are commonly cited as impacting peace duration. First, there is the role played by the presence of peacekeeping operations. As several scholars have noted, the presence of a peacekeeping operation in a post-conflict state significantly cuts the security costs of an organization and helps solidify credible commitment to a negotiated settlement, thus producing a more durable peace.[38] We use Paige Fortna's and Mason et al.'s extension of that data, *Peace Keeping Operation and Performance* (PKOP, hereafter) to measure the presence of an international peacekeeping force.[39] There has been some debate over the effects of peacekeeping, with some studies finding that peacekeeping fosters post-war peace duration, at least in the short term, and others who argue that such operations have no impact, or reduce the likelihood of the emergence of a durable peace.[40]

In addition, we include a number of domestic political, social, and economic control variables, all of which are cited in the literature as impacting peace duration. Some scholars have argued that political institution factors can affect both peace duration (and also the likelihood of post-war democracy).[41] In particular, scholars from the consociational tradition have argued that political institutions that increase inclusion of disparate political viewpoints and the development of consensualism (via the use proportional representation electoral systems) better promotes peace.[42] We coded countries in terms of whether countries employed some variation of proportional representation electoral system (or not) to govern post-conflict elections by year for the hazard analyses and by country for the FIRST post-conflict election for the logit analysis.

There are several social and economic control variables we employ in our analyses as well. First there is *Ethnic Fractionalization* that is used to measure the extent to which a society is ethnically divided (which can affect the durability of post-conflict peace). We use Montalvo and Reyna-Querol's ethnic fractionalization data.[43] As a measure of development we use Infant Mortality Rate (IMR) of a country, which measures the infrastructure capabilities of a state and also provides information as to the level of poverty. Due to the high level of variation in the infant mortality rate, we use logged IMR in the statistical models. We use the World Bank Data on Human Development for data on this measure. [44]

Many studies have also pointed to the "rentier" effect or how the natural resource "curse" contributes to civil war occurrence and recurrence.[45] From this perspective, natural resources provide incentives for capturing resources and restarting civil wars (or what some scholars have referred to as the "greed" motivation).[46] We use Michael Ross's data on the oil and gas production of a country. We take the logged value of gas and oil exports as a percentage of total exports as an indicator of dependence on resource exports.

Finally, there are the effects of the preceding civil war itself on the likelihood of civil war recurrence, especially civil war duration, intensity, and the type of civil war, although there is not much in the way of consensus as to the direction of these effects. Indeed, there have been contradictory findings regarding the impact of both the intensity and length of civil wars on the recurrence of civil wars. For instance, some argue that the cost of the civil war may affect the stability of the peace after the war is over, with more intense and violent wars leading to a greater likelihood of a resumption of conflict. Others have argued that the greater the intensity, the less likely combatants will restart a conflict (because they are fearful about the costs of resuming a war or conflict).[47] Still others have argued that the duration of a conflict may also affect the duration of peace following the conflict end. On the one hand, long-duration wars may signify the existence of an intractable conflict that is not easily resolved (but easily restarted). On the other hand, longer conflicts may lead to war weariness that promotes a greater likelihood of a durable peace.[48] To measure duration of a civil war we used data from Wallensteen and Pettersson[49] using a natural log of length in months of a civil war.[50] Finally, some suggest that identity wars (or those involving ethnicity or religion, as opposed to ideological wars) have very different causes and hence different implications for peace duration.[51] Thus, we coded the conflicts in our data set as either identity wars or not.

Analysis

To test the above hypotheses on the relationship between long-term inclusion and peace duration, we employ several empirical strategies. First, as is commonly used in the empirical literature on peace duration, we employ hazard modelling techniques. In medical science these techniques were used in examining the effectiveness of cancer treatments on patient survival. They are now widely used in political science and

FROM BULLETS TO BALLOTS

international relations, and are techniques that are particularly well suited for the study of civil war and civil conflict resumption.[52]

Generally two types of hazard analyses are commonly used in the social sciences: Weibull and Cox estimation techniques. In this analysis we use both techniques because each have their advocates and there is some debate as to which is the superior technique. In the health sciences, economics, and international relations, the Weibull technique is widely used.[53] Cox's proportional hazards regression technique is popular in political science, stemming largely from extensive experience in its application, and the fact that it is distribution free: no assumption needs to be made about the underlying distribution of survival times to make inferences about relative failure rates. The Cox model is a statistical method that produces a hazard rate that reflects "the risk an object incurs at any given moment in time, given an event has not occurred".[54] By estimating this model, we obtain a hazard rate of the occurrence of a civil war and civil conflict. An increase in the hazard rate suggests that there is an increase in the likelihood of a civil war or civil conflict, and a decrease in the hazard rate suggests there is a decrease in the likelihood of a recurrence of civil war.

To test for the proportionality assumption, which is especially important for Cox hazard models, the Schoenfeld residual-based test is recommended.[55] We conducted the test for non-proportionality for all models to determine which variables violated the proportionality assumption. Although some of the variables violated this assumption, we corrected for this by interacting these variables with time, a corrective commonly used when using hazard models.[56] In addition, to check for potential multicollinearity a Variance Inflation Factor (VIF) test was conducted. Most VIF scores are less than 2 for any of the explanatory variables, thus indicating that multicollinearity is not a problem for the analyses.[57] The exception is the relationship between the logged percent of legislative seats held by former rebel parties, and executive inclusion. Thus, we chose to run these variables in separate models reported in Table 2.

The second technique we employ is a basic binary logit model where, instead of estimating the likelihood of conflict recurrence in a given year, we code as the dependent variable whether a civil war in a country, or a civil conflict in a dyad, recurred within five years of the beginning of the peace. If conflict recurred we coded this as a "0", and if it did not we coded this as a "1" (for example, peace has persisted). Thus, in addition to estimating the likelihood a conflict would recur in a given year, we are also able to estimate whether peace in a country or a dyad "survived" (avoided a conflict for at least a five-year period).

Table 2 reports the results of conducting hazard analyses using both Weibull and Cox estimation techniques. Hazard ratios are interpreted differently from coefficients in a normal regression model: when a hazard ratio is larger than 1, this indicates the percent *increase* in the dependent variable (or in this case the likelihood of civil war or conflict recurrence); when the hazard ratio is below 1, this indicates the percent *decrease* in the likelihood of civil war or conflict recurrence. Further, since in the dyadic analysis, dyads are "nested" within country context, we cluster the robust standard errors by country to model in the multilevel nature of the data.

The results from eight models are reported with the first four models (1–4) reporting results regarding whether a civil war recurred in a given year for a country as a whole. The second set of models (5–8) report whether a conflict resumed in a government–former rebel party dyad. Since the logged percent of legislative seats held by all rebel groups was collinear with whether a former rebel party had access to the executive

48

Table 2. Dyadic and national-level peace duration analyses (hazard ratios and robust/robust clustered standard errors reported).

Variable	Model 1	Model 2	Model 3	Model 4	Model 5	Model 6	Model 7	Model 8
			National Level			Dyadic Level		
	Weibull HR (Robust standard errors)	Cox	Weibull	Cox	Weibull HR (Robust standard clustered errors)	Cox	Weibull	Cox
Logged %Seats	0.919 (.156)	1.066 (.128)			0.994 (.023)	1.007 (.012)		
Major Party Excluded	1.433*** (.117)	1.570*** (.134)	5.951*** (2.61)	4.881*** (1.95)				
Executive Inclusion			0.913 (.070)	0.996 (.068)			0.562^ (.197)	0.544* (.161)
UN Peacekeeping	0.848^ (.081)	0.911 (.067)	0.926 (.369)	0.974 (.368)	0.894^ (.062)	0.845*** (.044)	0.714* (.110)	0.761** (.081)
Prop. Representation	1.086 (.068)	1.277** (.087)	1.226* (.120)	1.303* (.153)	1.631 (.715)	1.503 (.513)	0.893 (.319)	0.974 (.283)
Ethnic Fractionalization	0.796 (.151)	0.565* (.127)	0.477* (.157)	0.414* (.190)	0.179*** (.043)	0.271*** (.049)	0.147*** (.077)	0.239*** (.079)
Infant Mortality	0.995*** (.001)	0.996*** (.001)	0.995*** (.002)	0.997*** (.001)	0.996*** (.001)	0.996*** (.001)	0.780*** (.039)	0.779*** (.029)
Logged Oil and Gas Production by Country (Exports)	1.284* (.163)	1.600*** (.206)	1.222** (.103)	1.302** (.134)	1.787* (.503)	1.791*** (.424)	1.233* (.131)	1.158* (.084)
Logged Battle Deaths	0.999 (.010)	0.974* (.013)	0.969*** (.011)	0.950*** (.014)	1.126 (.106)	1.091 (.087)	1.207* (.060)	1.135^ (.079)
Logged War Duration (Months)	0.836*** (.033)	0.775*** (.034)	0.543*** (.115)	0.660** (.124)	0.960** (.015)	0.934*** (.018)	0.917* (.016)	0.903*** (.025)
Identity War	2.451* (1.14)	2.599** (1.14)	1.189* (.092)	1.171* (.086)	5.367*** (2.32)	5.352*** (2.43)	3.844*** (1.61)	3.937*** (1.63)
Constant	0.018*** (.021)		0.174^ (.172)		0.009*** (.007)		0.060*** (.055)	
N (years)	602	602	602	602	1278	1278	1279	1279
Failures (civil war conflict recurrence years)	42	42	41	41	74	74	74	74
Wald χ^2	133.55	84.49	220.29	142.78	131.70	113.32	60.48	84.88

Statistical significance is reported at the 90% (^), 95% (*), 99% (**), and 99.5% (***) confidence levels (with the VIF score greater than 6 in this case), we ran models for legislative inclusion (models 1, 2, 5, and 6) separately from executive inclusion (models 3, 4, 7, 8). Further, to test hypothesis 1a above, whether or not all former rebel parties were included in the legislature affected the recurrence of civil war in a country, we only include this variable in the national level analysis.

The results from the hazard analysis reported in Table 2 do not indicate support for our first hypothesis, that legislative inclusion helps reduce the likelihood of conflict recurrence in dyads, nor does legislative representation reduce civil war recurrence in national level models. The relationships are not statistically significant, and the direction of the hazard ratios (in as much as they are close to "1") suggests the impact of legislative representation is substantively small. Thus, the overall level of representation in the legislature does not impact the likelihood of conflict resumption.

However, there is support for hypothesis 1a: when one or more significant former rebel parties are excluded, this dramatically increases the likelihood of civil war resumption. This result suggests that what matters most is not the level of representation in a legislature, but whether any *significant political actors are left out*. This supports the arguments made by scholars who suggest that inclusion in the short run prevents the emergence of "spoilers". Our results suggest that this is also the case in the long run. Exclusion from the legislature of any major relevant parties dramatically increases the likelihood of a recurrent civil war.

There is rather mixed support for hypothesis 2. For the national level results (reported in models 3 and 4 in Table 2) executive inclusion reduces the likelihood of national civil war by 1–9%, but the relationship is not statistically significant. This however could mean, when considering the result for legislative exclusion that executive inclusion may only include one of several parties, and others are excluded. This interpretation is also suggested by the results from the dyadic models (models 7 and 8). The likelihood of dyadic conflict resumption is significantly reduced by executive inclusion, by 44–46%.

The analyses from Table 2 also provide some support for previous theories regarding peace duration in post-conflict environments. Not surprisingly, we find a strong statistical association between the presence of United Nations Peacekeepers (UNPKO) and peace duration among dyads. Substantively, the presence of UNPKO decreases the likelihood of peace failure among dyads by 10–29%. However, the evidence does not strongly support the notion that UNPKO reduce the likelihood of civil war recurrence at the national level. Although all the hazard ratios are less than 1 in models 1, 2, 3, and 4 (suggesting a small reduction in the likelihood of civil war resumption in a given year), these relationships are not statistically significant.

In terms of the statistical and substantive relationship between power sharing institutions and peace duration, we find little consistent support that proportional representation systems are more or less likely to affect conflict resumption, although in the national level results these systems tend to be associated with a greater likelihood of civil war resumption. Ethnically fractionalized societies are associated with lower levels of civil war and conflict resumption. Interestingly among countries that have higher levels of infant mortality (or less developed countries) there is a lower likelihood of civil war and conflict resumption. Finally, the presence of oil and gas production increases the likelihood of civil war and conflict recurrence.

FROM BULLETS TO BALLOTS

Post-settlement states experiencing longer civil wars are associated with a lower likelihood of both civil war and conflict. This suggests support for the "war weariness" argument about the effects of the conflict on peace duration. The substantive effect of previous civil war duration reduces the likelihood of renewed civil war by 27–46% and the likelihood of conflict resumption in a dyad by 4–9%. Further, civil wars and conflicts that were previously identity wars have a very great likelihood of resuming after a settlement, although the intensity of the previous civil war (as measured by logged battle deaths) has a substantively small effect on the likelihood of civil war or conflict resumption.

Although many of the findings raised by the results from the control variables are themselves interesting and potentially provocative, they lie beyond the current scope of this article. Our focus is on whether inclusion tends to reduce the likelihood of civil war recurrence in a country and conflict recurrence in dyads. The above results suggest support in favour of the inclusion hypotheses.

However, to further check our hazard analyses results above, Table 3 reports the results from a set of simple logit analyses where the dependent variable is coded as whether at least five years of peace are maintained after a settlement. In many ways this approximates a "five year" survival rate to ascertain whether peace results from inclusion into the political process. In this case, if at least five years of peace (that is, absence of war and conflict) had occurred in a country or a dyad after a settlement, this is coded as a "1" and if war had recurred this is coded as a "0".

Table 3 reports odd ratios and robust standard errors (and robust clustered standard errors for the dyadic results since the dyads are nested within countries). It is important to note that odds ratios are interpreted differently than general coefficients. As with

Table 3. Binary logit analyses, five-year peace test using national and dyadic data, peace maintained for five years = 1 (odds ratios and robust/robust clustered standard errors reported).

Variable	National		Dyadic
	Model 9 Odds Ratio	Model 10 Odds Ratio	Model 11 Odds Ratio
Major Party Excluded	0.015***	0.016***	
	(.018)	(.019)	
Executive Inclusion	3.246^	3.355^	3.576**
	(2.21)	(1.30)	(.564)
UN Peacekeeping	1.921	1.363	1.601
	(1.46)	(.921)	(.399)
Prop. Representation		0.691	0.604
		(.497)	(.495)
Ethnic Fractionalization	0.191		21.278
	(.315)		(2.11)
Infant Mortality	0.998	1.001	1.000
	(.007)	(.007)	(.005)
Logged Oil and Gas Production by Country (Exports)	0.891***	0.900***	0.732**
	(.029)	(.029)	(.125)
Logged War Duration (Months)	1.671	1.935^	1.084
	(.648)	(.730)	(.151)
Identity War	0.091***	0.092***	0.211***
	(.062)	(.055)	(.441)
Constant	34.340^	7.454	0.768
	(68.2)	(13.3)	(.990)
N	69	69	118
Pseudo R²	0.455	0.427	0.185

hazard ratios, when an odds ratio is larger than 1, this indicates the percent *increase* in the dependent variable; when the odds ratio is below 1, this indicates the percent *decrease* in the dependent variable.

In addition, since in Table 2 above it was demonstrated that the logged percent of seats held by former rebel parties was unrelated to conflict recurrence (and because this variable was collinear with executive inclusion), in Table 3 we only included the executive inclusion and major party exclusion variables in the logit models. Also, since the proportional representation and ethnic fractionalization variables are highly collinear (VIF > 6) we ran two separate models (models 9 and 10) for the national level data.

As Table 3 reports, consistent with the results from the hazard analyses above, executive inclusion significantly increases the likelihood that peace survives five years after a settlement, for both civil wars at the national level, and civil conflict at the dyadic level. Further when a rebel party is excluded from legislative representation, this significantly decreases peace survival in a country. Within five years, the likelihood of peace when a party is excluded is reduced by about 98%.

Conclusion

This article, unlike others in this special issue that focus on the transformation of rebel groups into political actors, seeks to understand how the inclusion of former rebel organizations is associated with post-conflict peace duration. Indeed, our findings support much of the literature that argues inclusion in the short run (for example, in the negotiation process leading up to the peace settlement) is good for peace duration. This appears to be also the case in the long run. Including relevant rebel groups (and perhaps more importantly not excluding significant groups) reduces the likelihood of civil war and conflict resumption.

However, as we note above, what is really important is not the level of representation for former rebel parties, but that no major party is left out of the political process. Exclusion from legislative representation is strongly associated with civil war and conflict resumption. Although access to the executive also appears to dampen the likelihood of civil war and conflict resumption, the key factor is the non-exclusion of major former rebel parties from representation in governing institutions.

Of course, a key question yet unexplored is whether inclusion of former rebel parties leads to more democratic outcomes? Regarding this question, some of the other contributions in this special issue express a good degree of pessimism. Manning and Smith, for example, suggest that the successful transformation of rebel groups into political parties may not necessarily bode well for democracy, in as much as these parties often seek to create one-party states once attaining power (a point also echoed by Terrence Lyons).[58] On the other hand, the successful transformation and electoral success of the FMLN in El Salvador certainly has contributed to the deepening of democracy in that country. Perhaps whether or not inclusion leads to democratic outcomes may depend heavily on what type of rebel party emerges. Certainly there are distinct differences between the many "warlord" groups that make up many rebel groups in Africa, as compared to the revolutionary alliances found in places like El Salvador, Guatemala and Nepal. Although a potentially fruitful path for future research, this is beyond the scope of this current project, and will have to wait for a future iteration of this project.

FROM BULLETS TO BALLOTS

Notes

1. Manning, "Party-Building on the Heels of War"; de Zeeuw, *From Soldiers to Politicians*; Deonandan et al., *From Revolutionary Movements*; Söderberg- Kovacs, *From Rebellion to Politics*.
2. Ishiyama and Batta, "Swords into Plowshares."
3. Ishiyama and Marshall, "Candidate Recruitment."
4. Ishiyama and Widmeier, "Territorial Control"; Allison, "The Legacies of Violence"; Allison, "The Transition from Armed Opposition."
5. Suazo, "Tools of Change"; Joshi and Mason, "Civil War Settlements"; Stedman, "Peace Processes"; Stedman, "Spoiler Problems"; Blaydes and De Maio, "Spoiling the Peace?"
6. Ishiyama and Batta, "Swords into Plowshares"; Manning, "Party-Building on the Heels of War."
7. Gurses and Mason, "Democracy out of Anarchy"; Wantchekon and Jensen, "Bypassing Leviathan."
8. Suazo, "Tools of Change."
9. Stedman, "Peace Processes"; Stedman, "Spoiler Problems"; Blaydes and De Maio, "Spoiling the Peace?"
10. Suazo, "Tools of Change," 8.
11. In this article we focus on peace because, in many ways, peace is a necessary condition for democratization. Without some semblance of peace, democratization cannot occur (although of course peace does not guarantee democracy).
12. Hartzell, "Explaining the Stability"; Hartzell and Hoddie, "Institutionalizing Peace"; Walter, "The Critical Barrier"; Walter, *Committing to Peace*; Fortna, "Inside and Out"; Fortna, "Does Peacekeeping Keep Peace?"
13. Hampson, *Nurturing Peace*; Rubin, "The Actors in Negotiation."
14. Licklider, *Stopping the Killing,* 701.
15. Ohlson and Söderberg, "From Intra-State War"; Rubin, "The Actors in Negotiation."
16. Stedman, "Spoiler Problems"; Blaydes and De Maio, "Spoiling the Peace?"; Newman and Richmond, *Challenges to Peacebuilding*; Zahar, "Reframing the Spoiler Debate."
17. Hampson, *Nurturing Peace,* 217.
18. Nilsson, "Partial Peace," 481.
19. Hartzell, "Explaining the Stability."
20. Hartzell and Hoddie, "Institutionalizing Peace," 318.
21. Binningsbø, "Power-Sharing, Peace and Democracy."
22. Simonsen, "Addressing Ethnic Divisions."
23. Suazo, "Tools of Change," 24.
24. Ibid.
25. Ibid., 25.
26. Sambanis, "Do Ethnic and Non-Ethnic Civil Wars."
27. Cunningham et al., "It Takes Two"; Kreutz, "How and When Armed Conflicts End"; Fortna, "Does Peacekeeping Keep Peace?"
28. Eriksson and Wallensteen, "Armed Conflict 1989–2003"; Gleditsch et al., "Armed Conflict 1946–2001."
29. Mason et al., "When Civil Wars Recur"; Doyle and Sambanis, "International Peacebuilding"; Hartzell and Hoddie, "Institutionalizing Peace"; Collier and Hoeffler, "Greed and Grievance in Civil War."
30. Mason et al., "When Civil Wars Recur."
31. Stedman, "Spoiler Problems"; Blaydes and De Maio, "Spoiling the Peace?"; Newman and Richmond, *Challenges to Peacebuilding*; Zahar, "Reframing the Spoiler Debate."
32. Birnir, *Ethnicity and Electoral Politics*; Ishiyama, "Do Ethnic Parties Exacerbate Minority Ethnic Conflict."
33. Wallensteen and Pettersson, "Armed Conflicts."
34. From these settlements we identified 112 rebel organizations that were part of a peace settlement that ended the civil war. Of these, 59 became political parties for the first general election following negotiated settlements (or 118 dyads). This accounts for 52% of the total number of former rebel organizations. The remaining organizations either merged with other established parties, or dissolved, or became criminal enterprises, or returned to armed rebellion before the first election.

FROM BULLETS TO BALLOTS

35. It is important to note here that many of these groups either disappeared or merged with other parties. Our focus in this study is only on the organizations that became parties. As with other articles in this special issue, we use a minimal definition of party, based upon Anthony Downs, as a group that runs for election under a particular and unique label. Downs, *An Economic Theory*.
    A list of former rebel party organizations at the time of the signing of the peace settlement is available from the authors upon request.
36. Data on representation was standardized so that parties with zero representation would not be undefined. Log (Number of Seats + 1)
37. Golder and Bormann, "Democratic Electoral Systems"; Nohlen et al., *Elections in Africa*; Sagar, *Political Parties of the World.*
38. Walter, *Committing to Peace.*
39. Fortna, "Inside and Out."
40. Wantchekon and Jensen, "Bypassing Leviathan"; Doyle and Sambanis, "International Peacebuilding."
41. Brancati, "Decentralization"; Dubey, "Domestic Institutions and the Duration of Civil War Settlements."
42. Lijphart, *Democracy in Plural Societies.*
43. Montalvo and Reyna-Querol, "Ethnic Polarization, Potential Conflict, and Civil Wars."
44. World Bank, *World Development Indicators.*
45. Collier and Hoeffler, "Greed and Grievance in Civil War"; Ross, "What Do We Know About Natural Resources and Civil War?"
46. Weinstein, *Inside Rebellion.*
47. Doyle and Sambanis, "International Peacebuilding"; Dubey, "Domestic Institutions and the Duration of Civil War Settlements."
48. Doyle and Sambanis, "International Peacebuilding". See also Hartzell et al., "Stabilizing the Peace"; Fortna and Huang, "Democratization after Civil War"; Gurses and Mason, "Democracy out of Anarchy"; Sambanis, "Do Ethnic and Non-Ethnic Civil Wars."
49. Wallensteen and Pettersson, "Armed Conflicts, 1946–2014."
50. Mason et al., "When Civil Wars Recur."
51. Sambanis, "Do Ethnic and Non-Ethnic Civil Wars."
52. Carroll, "On the Use and Utility of the Weibull Model"; Box-Steffensmeier and Jones, *Event History Modeling*; Mason et al., "When Civil Wars Recur."
53. Carroll, "On the Use and Utility of the Weibull Model"; Werner, "The Precarious Nature of Peace."
54. Box-Steffensmeier and Jones, *Event History Modeling*, 1419.
55. Box-Steffensmeier et al., "Nonproportional Hazards," 35.
56. Ibid. Several variables violated the Cox non-proportional hazard test. To correct these violations, the variables were interacted with time (t). These included the proportional representation variable, the ethnic fractionalization variable, whether the war was an identity war, the UNPKO dummy variable and Log of Battle Deaths in the previous civil war. We conducted Schoenfeld Residual Tests to determine which variables violated the hazard assumptions. The authors will provided the results for the Schoenfeld residual tests for each set of models upon request.
57. All models report Odds Ratios and Robust Clustered Standard Errors (RCSE). Statistical significance is reported at the 90% (*), 95% (**), and 99% (***) confidence levels.
58. Manning and Smith, "Political Party Formation"; Lyons, "From Victorious Rebels to Strong Authoritarian Parties."

Disclosure statement

No potential conflict of interest was reported by the authors.

FROM BULLETS TO BALLOTS

Bibliography

Allison, Michael. "The Legacy of Violence on Post-Civil War Elections: The Case of El Salvador." *Studies in Comparative International Development* 45, no. 1 (2010): 104–124.

Allison, Michael. "The Transition from Armed Opposition to Electoral Opposition in Central America." *Latin American Politics and Societies* 48, no. 1 (2006): 137–162.

Birnir, Johanna. *Ethnicity and Electoral Politics.* New York: Cambridge University Press, 2007.

Brancati, Dawn. "Decentralization: Fueling the Fire or Dampening the Flames of Ethnic Conflict and. Secessionism." *International Organization* 60, no. 3 (2006): 651–685.

Binningsbø, H. M. "Power-Sharing, Peace and Democracy: Any Obvious Relationship?" *International Areas Studies Review* 16, no. 1 (2013): 89–112.

Blaydes, Lisa and Jennifer De Maio. "Spoiling the Peace? Peace Process Exclusivity and Political Violence in North-Central Africa." *Civil Wars* 12, nos. 1–2 (2010): 3–28.

Box-Steffensmeier, Janet M. and Christopher Zorn. "Duration Models and Proportional Hazards in Political Science." *American Journal of Political Science* 45, no. 4 (2001): 972–988.

Box-Steffensmeier, Janet M., Dan Reiter, and Christopher Zorn. "Nonproportional Hazards and Event History Analysis in International Relations." *Journal of Conflict Resolution* 47, no. 1 (2003): 33–53.

Box-Steffensmeier, Janet M. and Bradford S. Jones. *Event History Modeling – A Guide for Social Scientists.* New York: Cambridge University Press, 2004.

Carroll, Kevin J. "On the Use and Utility of the Weibull Model in the Analysis of Survival Data." *Controlled Clinical Trials* 24, no. 6 (2003): 682–701.

Collier, Paul, and Anke Hoeffler. "Greed and Grievance in Civil War." *Oxford Economic Papers* 56, no. 4 (2004): 563–95.

Cunningham, David E., Kristian Skrede Gleditsch and Idean Salehyan. "It Takes Two: A Dyadic Analysis of Civil War Duration and Outcome." *Journal of Conflict Resolution* 53, no. 4 (2009): 570–597.

Deonandan, K., D. Close, G. Prevost, eds. *From Revolutionary Movements to Political Parties.* New York: Palgrave MacMillan, 2007.

Doyle, Michael and Nicholas Sambanis. "International Peacebuilding: A Theoretical and Quantitative Analysis." *American Political Science Review* 94, no. 4 (2000): 779–801.

Dubey, A. "Domestic Institutions and the Duration of Civil War Settlements." Paper presented at the Annual Meeting of the International Studies Association, March 24–27, 2002. New Orleans.

Downs, Anthony. *An Economic Theory of Democracy.* New York: Harper and Row, 1957.

Eriksson, Mikael, and Peter Wallensteen. "Armed Conflict, 1989–2003." *Journal of Peace Research* 41, no. 5 (2004): 625–636.

Fortna, Virginia Page. "Inside and Out: Peacekeeping and the Duration of Peace after Civil and Interstate Wars." *International Studies Review* 5, no. 4 (2003): 97–114.

Fortna, Virginia Page. "Does Peacekeeping Keep Peace? International Intervention and the Duration of Peace after Civil War." *International Studies Quarterly* 48, no. 2 (2004): 269–92.

Fortna, Virginia Page and Reyko Huang. "Democratization after Civil War: A Brush-Clearing Exercise." *International Studies Quarterly* 56, no. 4 (2012): 801–808.

Gleditsch, Nils Petter, Peter Wallensteen, Mikael Eriksson, Margareta Sollenberg, and Havard Strand. "Armed Conflict 1946-2001: A New Dataset." *Journal of Peace Research* 39, no. 5 (2002): 615–637.

Golder, Matt and Nils-Christian Bormann. "Democratic Electoral Systems around the World 1946–2011." *Electoral Studies* 32, no. 1 (2013): 360–369.

Gurses, Mehmet, and T. David Mason. "Democracy out of Anarchy: The Prospects for Post-Civil-War Democracy." *Social Science Quarterly* 89, no. 2 (2008): 315–36.

Hampson, Fen Osler. *Nurturing Peace: Why Peace Settlements Succeed or Fail.* Washington, D.C. United States Institute of Peace Press, 1996.

FROM BULLETS TO BALLOTS

Hartzell, Caroline A. "Explaining the Stability of Negotiated Settlements to Intrastate Wars." *Journal of Conflict Resolution* 43, no. 1 (1999): 3–22.

Hartzell, Caroline, and Matthew Hoddie. "Institutionalizing Peace: Power Sharing and Post-Civil War Conflict Management." *American Journal of Political Science* 47, no. 2 (2003): 318–332.

Hartzell, Caroline, Matthew Hoddie, and Donald Rothchild. "Stabilizing the Peace after Civil War: An Investigation of Some Key Variables." *International Organization* 55, no. 4 (2001): 183–208.

Ishiyama, John. "Do Ethnic Parties Exacerbate Minority Ethnic Conflict?" *Nationalism and Ethnic Politics* 15, no. 3 (2009): 56–83.

Ishiyama, John and Anna Batta. "Swords into Plowshares: The Organizational Transformation of Rebel Groups into Political Parties." *Communist and Post-Communist Studies* 44, no. 2 (2011): 369–379.

Ishiyama, John and Michael Marshall. "Candidate Recruitment and Former Rebel Parties." *Party Politics* 21, no. 4 (2015): 591–602.

Ishiyama, John and Michael Widmeier. "Territorial Control, Level of Violence, and the Electoral Performance of Former Rebel Political Parties after Civil Wars." *Civil Wars* 15, no. 4 (2013): 521–550.

Joshi, Madhav and T. David Mason. "Civil War Settlements, Size of Governing Coalition, and Durability of Peace in Post-Civil War States." *International Interactions* 37, no. 4 (2011): 388–413.

Kreutz, Joakim. "How and When Armed Conflicts End: Introducing the UCDP Conflict Termination Dataset." *Journal of Peace Research* 47, no. 2 (2010): 243–250.

Licklider, Roy, ed. *Stopping the Killing: How Civil Wars End.* New York and London: New York University Press, 1993.

Lijphart, Arend. *Democracy in Plural Societies: A Comparative Exploration.* New Haven: Yale University Press, 1977.

Lyons, Terrence. "From Victorious Rebels to Strong Authoritarian Parties: Prospects for Post-War Democratization." *Democratization* 23, no. 6: 1038–1056.

Manning, Carrie. "Party-Building on the Heels of War: El Salvador, Bosnia, Kosovo and Mozambique." *Democratization* 14, no. 1 (2007): 1–20.

Manning, Carrie and Ian Smith. "Political Party Formation by Former Armed Opposition Groups after Civil War." *Democratization* 23, no. 6: 972–997.

Mason, David, Patrick Brandt, Mehmet Gurses, and Jason M. Quinn. "When Civil Wars Recur: Conditions for Durable Peace after Civil Wars." *International Studies Perspectives* 12, no. 2 (2011): 171–189.

Montalvo Jose, G. and Marta Reyna-Querol. "Ethnic Polarization, Potential Conflict, and Civil Wars." *American Economic Review* 95, no. 3 (2005): 797–816.

Newman, Edward, and Oliver Richmond. *Challenges to Peacebuilding: Managing Spoilers During Conflict Resolution.* Tokyo: United Nations University Press, 2006.

Nilsson, Desirée. "Partial Peace: Rebel Groups Inside and Outside of Civil War Settlements." *Journal of Peace Research* 45, no. 4 (2008): 479–495.

Nohlen, Dieter, Michael Krennerich, and Berhard Thibaut. *Elections in Africa: A Data Handbook.* Oxford: Oxford University Press, 2012.

Ohlson, Thomas, and Mimmi Söderberg. "From Intra-State War To Democratic Peace in Weak States." In *Uppsala Peace Research Papers*, 1–35. Uppsala: Department of Peace and Conflict Research, Uppsala University, 2002.

Ross, Michael L. "What Do We Know About Natural Resources and Civil War?." *Journal of Peace Research* 41, no. 3 (2004): 337–56.

Rubin, Jeffrey Z. "The Actors in Negotiation." In *International Negotiation: Analysis, Approaches, Issues, Second Edition*, edited by V. A. Kremenyuk, 97–109. San Francisco: Jossey-Bass, 2002.

Sagar, D.J., ed. *Political Parties of the World.* Farmington: John Harper Publishing Inc, 2009.

Sambanis, Nicholas. "Do Ethnic and Non-Ethnic Civil Wars Have the Same Causes? A Theoretical and Empirical Inquiry (Part I)." *Journal of Conflict Resolution* 45, no. 3 (2001): 259–82.

Simonsen, Sven Gunnar. "Addressing Ethnic Divisions in Post-Conflict Institution-Building: Lessons from Recent Cases." *Security Dialogue* 36, no. 3 (2005): 297–318.

Söderberg- Kovacs, M. *From Rebellion to Politics.* Stockholm: Uppsala Universitet, 2007.

Stedman, Stephen John. "Peace Processes and the Challenges of Violence." In *Contemporary Peacemaking: Conflict, Peace Processes and Post-War Reconstruction*, edited by John Darby and Roger McGinty, 147–158. London: Palgrave, 2008.

FROM BULLETS TO BALLOTS

Stedman, Stephen John. "Spoiler Problems in Peace Processes." *International Security* 22, no. 2 (1997): 5–53.

Suazo, Adan E. "Tools of Change: Long-Term Inclusion in Peace Processes." *PRAXIS The Fletcher Journal of Human Security* 28, no. 1 (2013): 5–27.

Wallensteen, Peter and Therese Pettersson. "Armed Conflicts, 1946–2014." *Journal of Peace Research* 52, no. 4 (2014): 536–550.

Walter, Barbara F. "The Critical Barrier to Civil War Settlement." *International Organization* 51, no. 3 (1997): 335–64.

Walter, Barbara F. *Committing to Peace: The Successful Settlement of Civil Wars*. Princeton and Oxford: Princeton University Press, 2002.

Wantchekon, Leonard, and Nathan M. Jensen. "Bypassing Leviathan: The Unlikely Emergence of Democracy out of Civil War." New York University and Washington University, unpublished manuscript, 2009.

Weinstein, Jeremy M. *Inside Rebellion: The Politics of Insurgent Violence*. New York, NY: Cambridge University Press, 2007.

Werner, Suzanne. "The Precarious Nature of Peace: Resolving the Issues, Enforcing the Settlement, and Renegotiating the Terms." *American Journal of Political Science* 43, no. 2 (1999): 912–934.

World Bank. *World Development Indicators*. Accessed December 10, 2015. http://data.worldbank.org/indicator. 2015.

Zahar, Marie-Joëlle. "Reframing the Spoiler Debate in Peace Processes." In *Contemporary Peacemaking: Conflict, Violence and Peace Processes*, edited by J. Darby and R. Mac Ginty, 159–177. London: Palgrave Macmillan, 2003.

de Zeeuw, Jeroun, ed. *From Soldiers to Politicians: Transforming Rebel Movements after Civil War*. Boulder: Lynne Reinner, 2007.

From victorious rebels to strong authoritarian parties: prospects for post-war democratization

Terrence Lyons

School for Conflict Analysis and Resolution, George Mason University, Arlington, USA

ABSTRACT
In a number of cases, rebel movements that won civil wars transformed into powerful authoritarian political parties that dominated post-war politics. Parties whose origins are as victorious insurgent groups have different legacies and hence different institutional structures and patterns of behaviour than those that originated in breakaway factions of ruling parties, labour unions, non-violent social movements, or identity groups. Unlike classic definitions of political parties, post-rebel parties are not created around the need to win elections but rather as military organizations focused on winning an armed struggle. Key attributes of victorious rebel movements, such as cohesive leadership, discipline, hierarchy, and patterns of military administration of liberated territory, shape post-insurgent political parties and help explain why post-insurgent parties are often strong and authoritarian. This article seeks to identify the mechanisms that link rebel victory in three East African countries (Uganda, Ethiopia, and Rwanda) to post-war authoritarian rule. These processes suggest that how a civil war ends changes the potential for post-war democratization.

Introduction

In a number of cases, rebel movements that won civil wars transformed into powerful authoritarian political parties that dominated post-war politics. Parties whose origins are as victorious insurgent groups have different legacies and hence different institutional structures and patterns of behaviour than those that originated in breakaway factions of ruling parties, labour unions, non-violent social movements, or identity groups.[1] The strength and durability of a political party, Huntington suggested, "derives more from its origins than from its character".[2] Unlike classic definitions of political parties, post-rebel parties are not created around the need to win elections but rather as military organizations focused on winning an armed struggle.[3] Key attributes of victorious rebel movements, such as cohesive leadership, discipline, hierarchy, and patterns of military administration of liberated territory, shape post-insurgent political parties and help explain why post-insurgent parties are often strong and authoritarian. This article seeks to identify the mechanisms that link rebel victory in three East

African countries (Uganda, Ethiopia, and Rwanda) to post-war authoritarian rule. These processes suggest that how a civil war ends changes the potential for post-war democratization.

After this introduction, the second section of this article reviews recent research on war-to-peace transitions and on the roles played by political parties in authoritarian regimes. It then examines how insurgent groups operate as proto-political parties during the period of armed struggle and how legacies of wartime shape the nature of the post-war democratization. The third section uses the three East African cases to identify a mechanism that links the rebel movement to the post-war authoritarian party. This mechanism includes leadership coherence and discipline, the legacies of wartime administration of liberated territory, and the opportunities in the transition from war to peace to consolidate power. The final concluding section develops some of the implications of these findings and thoughts regarding future research.

Transforming rebel movements into political parties

There has been a significant growth in research on the transformation of rebel movements into political parties. Until recently scholars of political parties paid relatively little attention to cases following civil war and the conflict resolution community said little about the roles played by post-conflict parties in promoting peacebuilding. Manning's early work on Mozambique provides an important case study of the transformation of the Renamo rebel movement in Mozambique.[4] Ishiyama and Batta point to the links between the organizational legacies of civil war and centripetal dynamics within new post-war parties.[5] Lyons emphasizes how processes to "demilitarize politics" can promote post-war parties that are able to operate effectively within the context of electoral competition.[6] Most of this scholarship focuses on transitions following negotiated settlements and where the international community played an important role in supporting "liberal peacebuilding".[7] What has been missing from this literature, however, has been a consideration of cases where the insurgent force won the war. The war-to-peace transition following rebel victory is different than the transition in cases of a negotiated settlement with important implications for the character of post-war parties and prospects for democratization.

The existing literature on the links between war termination by victory and post-war politics provides inconsistent findings. Toft argues that civil wars that end in rebel victory are more inclined to produce democratic outcomes. This, she suggests, is because victorious insurgents have both the military capability to penalize spoilers and the incentives to govern justly in order to gain legitimacy from both domestic constituencies and the international community. Following the logic of Tilly and the state-building literature, Toft argues that a "victor's peace" will lead to stronger institutions which in turn lead to "a more stable, and perhaps more democratic, system of government".[8] Negotiated settlements, she argues in contrast, are more likely to lead to renewed violence and to increased authoritarianism as weak governments crack down on the opposition. Weinstein also suggests that popular mobilization by the National Resistance Army (NRA) during the Ugandan civil war created the conditions for post-conflict democratization.[9] Fortna and Huang, however, find little support in the quantitative data for the hypothesis that military victories – including insurgent victories – improve the prospects for democratization.[10]

The argument in this article is that there is a specific type of strong authoritarian party that is the progeny of a victorious insurgent group. This is consistent with Levitsky and Way, who argue that strong authoritarian parties tend to be mass-based and often have high levels of solidarity derived from their origins in armed conflict.[11] Party "cohesion" is demonstrated by the leadership's ability to secure the cooperation of political allies or to impose discipline and therefore see less elite defection in times of crisis.[12] Other scholars have argued that one-party authoritarian regimes are likely to be stable and resist both international and domestic pressures to democratize.[13]

It is notable that three of the most powerful authoritarian ruling parties in Africa operate in states where protracted civil wars ended in rebel victory. These parties are not just networks supporting personal rulers or window dressing for military regimes. While neo-patrimonial links and ethnic mobilization are important, these post-insurgent political parties are distinguished from other African political parties by the legacies of winning their protracted civil wars. In Uganda, the National Resistance Movement (NRM) came to power in 1985 and has ruled first through a "no party" system and since 2005 through a multi-party system where the government dominated by the former insurgent force suppressed the opposition. In Ethiopia, the Ethiopian Peoples' Revolutionary Democratic Front (EPRDF) defeated the previous military regime in 1991 and, with the exception of 2005, held a series of non-competitive elections. The EPRDF won 100% of the seats in the 2015 national elections. The Rwandan Patriotic Front (RPF) came to power following the 1994 genocide and has ruled in a highly authoritarian manner that has prevented opposition from mobilizing or elections from being meaningful. In 2015, 98% of voters approved a referendum to amend the Rwandan constitution so that President Paul Kagame could run for re-election. These post-insurgent parties have used the legacies of the war and the processes of war-to-peace transitions to create the kind of strong authoritarian parties that have dominated post-war politics.

Political life during wartime: insurgents as proto-political parties

In order to survive in the harsh environment of protracted civil war, rebel groups must concurrently operate as private military organizations, have the ability to raise funds, and function in ways similar to peacetime political parties. As Collier and his colleagues argue, a successful rebel group is simultaneously a political party, a military organization, and a business.[14] Southall emphasizes the legacies of violence that shape politics during armed struggle: "War is violent, and the use of violence in politics comes at the expense of the gentler virtues which make for a good society."[15] In particular, launching an armed struggle reinforces hierarchy at the expense of internal democracy and the treatment of rival organizations as traitors rather than legitimate competitors.

Political organizations in the context of civil wars respond to a specific set of incentives and opportunities. The presence of protracted violence leads to specific forms of governance in the form of norms, expectations, and patterns of behaviour that shape perceptions of what is politically possible and thereby create the political context in which strategies are considered and adopted. Wartime governance is not anarchy and, as Menkhaus argues in the context of Somalia, there can be "governance without government".[16] War destroys many types of political institutions but provides the setting for others to thrive.[17] New research investigates different forms of what

Staniland calls "wartime political orders" as insurgents and states develop relationships during protracted armed struggle that are both cooperative and conflictual.[18]

Insurgent groups often arise in the context of brutal authoritarian regimes and therefore are characterized from their creation by secrecy and fear of betrayal. Della Porta's comparative work on clandestine political violence emphasizes the specific nature of solidarity that arises from underground politics.[19] Clandestine organizations tend to be particularly centralized, hierarchical, and compartmentalized and become more so as repression and violence escalate.

Other types of violence – communal conflicts, pogroms, urban riots – may not require a high level of institutionalization and may reflect a relatively unorganized, spontaneous outpouring of grievance-driven frustration or anger. Protracted civil wars such as those in Uganda, Ethiopia, and Rwanda, however, require institutions with highly developed capacities and structures to mobilize supporters and provision armed forces. Insurgent groups are generally studied as military organizations and more recently as greedy mafia-style business enterprises that are motivated by greed and the opportunities of illicit diamond mining or narcotics trafficking.[20] In the context of civil war, political organizations may perceive armed struggle rather than electoral competition as the most feasible tactic to achieve their political goals. Operating as an insurgency seeking military victory rather than as a party focused on electoral politics may therefore be a tactical response to the incentives of wartime rather than an inherent part of a movement's nature.

What is less often considered is how insurgent groups may be studied as proto-political parties and how rebels must overcome some of the same challenges as any other political party. In other words, while they differ with relation to the use of violence, "insurgent group" and "political party" play similar functions regarding mobilization in pursuit of political power. Rebels may differ from a classic definition of a political party as "a team seeking to control the governing apparatus by gaining office in a duly constituted election" but primarily in the tactics used in pursuit of the levers of power.[21] In this formulation, civil war is a form of contentious politics that requires a particular type of organization: the insurgent group.[22] The internal dynamics of alliance building and fragmentation of rebel movements is another way of understanding political processes during violent conflict.[23]

Linking victorious rebel groups to powerful authoritarian parties

This section traces how the nature of post-conflict political parties and their potential to promote democratization are shaped by their wartime legacies. In Uganda, Ethiopia, and Rwanda, small cohesive cohorts of leaders created insurgent movements based on strict discipline and hierarchical authority. In addition, experiences in military administration of liberated territory during the war form precedents and patterns of behaviour that are carried through the transition to peace. Political parties that originate in rebel movements often have particular characteristics that make it more likely that they will become powerful peacetime authoritarian parties and limit potential for democratization.

Wartime institutions: leadership coherence, discipline, and hierarchy

In Uganda, Ethiopia, and Rwanda, the leadership of the victorious insurgent groups had experience in politics before launching their rebellions. NRM leader Yoweri Museveni and several of his top leaders participated in the Uganda Patriotic Movement, a political party that competed in the 1980 elections. The leadership of the EPRDF first engaged in contentious politics as members of the student movement that sparked the Ethiopian revolution in the early 1970s and only later took up the armed struggle. Paul Kagame and several others in the leadership of the RPF engaged in politics through the Rwandan Alliance of National Unity, a diaspora-based political party. It was only after trying other political strategies and failing (often to face brutal repression) that these groups opted for armed struggle. Post-insurgent parties such as the NRM, EPRDF, and RPF therefore often had some form of existence as suppressed political movements prior to transforming into a rebel movement. In these cases and as political opportunities shifted, failed political parties became victorious rebels that then became powerful authoritarian ruling parties.

Insurgencies often begin with a small, dedicated group of committed fighters. According to official narratives, the NRA in Uganda launched the war with 27 men with guns, the Tigray People's Liberation Front (TPLF, the core of the EPRDF) with less than 100 fighters, and the RPF developed out of the Rwandan Alliance of National Unity that had just 100 members in 1983.[24] Early divisions and factionalization are either settled (often through violence) or differences are put aside (for a time) as the prospects for victory are realized. The pressures of protracted conflict forge relationships based on interdependence if not trust among leaders and between leaders and the rank-and-file. A coterie of linked leaders and high levels of solidarity forged in wartime facilitate the transition from a rebel movement to a strong authoritarian political party.

The early leaders of the NRA in Uganda had already struggled together in the Ugandan Patriotic Movement, a political party that had participated in the elections of 1980 before heading to the bush. The NRA's leadership was largely from the south-west of the country (particularly the Ankole). A number of Museveni's relatives joined him in the NRA, reinforcing the solidarity typical of clandestine networks and military units.[25] The rebel movement cannot be explained as a narrow ethnic organization because its main area of military operations was in the Buganda-inhabited Luweero triangle to the north of Kampala. The struggle was extremely violent, with an estimated 100,000–200,000 persons killed in a very small area.[26] This limited area and the high level of violence compelled the NRA to form a disciplined organization or perish. The NRA had no foreign border or inaccessible mountains to retreat to and therefore had a great fear of betrayal and infiltration, resulting in a well-articulated core leadership.[27]

During the protracted civil war in Ethiopia, the TPLF similarly developed a cohesive leadership and a disciplined, hierarchical organization.[28] The TPLF became the most powerful insurgent force in the northern Ethiopian region of Tigray only after defeating rival rebels in the Ethiopian Democratic Union and the Ethiopian People's Revolutionary Party in a series of pitched battles in the 1970s. In the late 1970s the TPLF faced splits and fissures in a period known as *hinfishfish* ("anarchy") that resulted in many deserting the movement and some dissenters being executed. As Milkias notes, the TPLF had strict discipline and made its decisions according to the precepts of democratic centralism so that "once policies were adopted, power was intended to flow only downward".[29] Meles Zenawi and a small group of others in the leadership formed the Marxist-Leninist League of Tigray (MLLT) in the mid-1980s, a tightly integrated vanguard within the TPLF, and it was this coterie that led the movement to victory. Another period of internal factionalization occurred in 1989 as war aims shifted following the liberation of Tigray. Many fighters returned to their villages rather than remain in the Front as it moved through non-Tigrayan areas towards Addis Ababa.[30] The TPLF was not cohesive by birth but became so over time as a core leadership in the MLLT consolidated its hold and purged the movement of dissent.

The early leaders of the RPF also had prior experience together in the Rwandan Alliance for National Unity, an organization of exiled politicians. Under Obote's regime in Uganda, Rwandan refugees were targeted and many joined Museveni in the NRA for self-defence, forging additional ties. The RPF began with an already established set of seasoned military leaders who had fought together in Uganda. Key leaders such as Fred Rwigyema and Paul Kagame were part of the group of 27 that were with Museveni when he started his insurgency in 1981. Rwigyema rose to deputy commander of the NRA before becoming commander of the RPF and Kagame served as head of military intelligence and was in the United States receiving training as an officer of the NRA when the civil war broke out.[31] The RPF therefore had a coherent military leadership and a battle-hardened army before it even stepped over the border into Rwanda in October 1990.

These illustrations therefore help us identify one possible mechanism that explains how victorious insurgent groups become powerful authoritarian political parties. In Uganda, Ethiopia, and Rwanda the rebels had coherent and disciplined leadership when they seized victory and began the process of transforming into a political party. This kind of leadership structure is in part the outcome of overcoming factionalization during the armed struggle and that contributed to the rebellion's success. In other words, post-insurgent parties often have particular attributes and leadership characteristics that developed not in the context of peaceful political competition nor as a result of the imperatives of winning elections but in the quite distinct context of violent, zero-sum, military struggles.

Liberated territory administration: legacies of military rule

Victorious insurgent groups often have direct experience administering liberated territory during the civil war. These wars are often protracted and therefore often attract what Balcells and Kalyvas call "higher quality rebels with the capacity to develop strong relations with civilian populations and build resilient institutions of governance".[32] Insurgents engaged in protracted warfare often provide governance in the form of public goods in order to secure the support of civilians in occupied territory. In some cases, rebels do more than control violence but seek to provide some level of public goods – a "rebelocracy" in Arjona typology.[33]

In this way insurgents, and particularly victorious rebels in protracted asymmetric conflict, have experience in performing functions of political administration. During civil war, military structures play roles that political parties fulfil in peacetime. Victorious insurgent groups often carry these models and precedents of military governance into the post-war political arena. The need to administer liberated territory provides incentives to develop cadres with skills to mobilize civilians under the difficult circumstances of violence and insecurity with the goal of supporting a military strategy. Not surprisingly, these precedents shape post-war governance as successful military administrators are converted (at least formally) into peacetime governors.

FROM BULLETS TO BALLOTS

The Ugandan NRA organized the population in areas it controlled during the war through "Resistance Councils" (RCs). The rebels generally treated civilians in liberated territory well and the RCs were in some measure a form of village democracy that reflected local opinion and grievances.[34] When military conditions contradicted local democracy, however, the NRA put military survival ahead of civilian protection. The RCs themselves were an improvisation to wartime conditions. According to one NRA member, the insurgents set up the RCs as military auxiliaries "out of necessity to survive during the war".[35] The *Uganda Resistance News* (NRA's wartime publication) emphasized the military importance of RCs:

> Although the committees were operating initially clandestinely, they succeeded in mobilizing the public towards the war effort. Their role was inter alia to provide information about the enemy's activities, movements and report his agents among the society. RCs also obtained foodstuffs and provided camping sites for the troops.[36]

The exigencies of administering liberated territory in support of an armed movement therefore shaped the NRA's experiences and the models it then transferred to local political structures after the war ended. When the NRA seized power in 1985, RCs were well-established in western Uganda, where the NRA controlled territory, and were put in place elsewhere around the country by 1987.

In northern Ethiopia, the TPLF saw itself as a classic Maoist-style guerrilla army that would win by forging relationships with the peasants of Tigray. In the very beginning of the civil war, however, the insurgent leaders from the cities needed the local knowledge of the peasants to survive.[37] In 1985 key leaders formed the MLLT, a vanguard party within the liberation front. As argued by Lenin in *What is to Be Done?*, the MLLT saw itself as a party of enlightened elites that could lead the masses to revolution.[38]

The TPLF was a political army that emphasized indoctrination and the military being under the control of the political party. Senior military leaders argued that armies are inherently political and what differentiates revolutionary militaries is the political order they serve. The rebels deployed political cadres with their military units to insure discipline and organize regular self-criticism sessions known as *gimgema*.[39] Local councils known as *bayto* ("peoples' council") worked under TPLF guidance to administer liberated zones. The *bayto* provided a mechanism for top-down wartime governance and served to implement the TPLF's war policies and "generate the maximum contribution to the movement's project" according to one of the founders of the TPLF.[40] Civilian administration supported the military agenda, and health workers and local administrators in liberated zones were regarded as "fighters" in the "people's struggle".[41]

During the famine of the mid-1980s, the Front had the capacity and local legitimacy to organize a massive movement of the population from Tigray to TPLF-controlled camps in Sudan.[42] The movement had its own very impressive humanitarian wing, the Relief Society of Tigray that coordinated large-scale relief operations with international assistance, and the Tigray Development Association that raised significant resources in the diaspora. The insurgents played other state-like diplomatic roles, including having extensive (and often contentious) relationships with neighbouring insurgents in Eritrea as well as a range of international actors and organizations.[43]

The TPLF therefore had extensive local political structures prior to gaining power, and these models developed during wartime shaped the design of post-war institutions. The rebels began the transition in 1991 with not only a large and battle-hardened

FROM BULLETS TO BALLOTS

military and a disciplined leadership but also cadres in every village in Tigray who were well integrated into a region-wide political network and with experience in administering liberated territory and managing top-down relationships with the peasantry. The TPLF effectively administered a mini-state before it seized power and took control over all of Ethiopia.

The RPF planned and organized their invasion of Rwanda for three years prior to crossing the border and anticipated a protracted civil war similar to the one many of them had experienced in Uganda.[44] The RPF occupied a liberated zone along Rwanda's border with Uganda but did not control significant territory until late 1992. Under military pressure in 1990–1991 the rebels retreated to the inaccessible Virunga Mountains to rearm and reorganize. A Ugandan journalist who visited territory controlled by the RPF in December 1992, during the ceasefire and lengthy peace talks in Arusha, reported that the insurgents "did a lot of political work with the civilian population trapped or freely living in rebel territory". Following models developed in the Luweero Triangle during the war in Uganda, the Rwandan rebels established "safe villages, where internally displaced people were mobilized, resettled, and empowered with political education".[45] While it lacked the extended experience administering liberated territory that characterized the rebels in Tigray and Uganda, the Rwandans had significant wartime experience fighting within the NRA. Kagame headed the NRA's military intelligence, providing him with valuable experience in maintaining discipline and detecting defection. Refugee camps and the large Rwandan population within the diaspora provided additional opportunities to develop skills and institutions to manage civilians in support of the military campaign.

After victory: legitimacy and transforming insurgent groups into political parties

Victorious rebels are more likely to derive significant legitimacy from defeating the old order and ending the violence – "we rule because we won!" Rebels who fight to stalemate and accept negotiations can claim a role in forcing a transition but those claims are more ambivalent and contingent than claims of unilateral victory. War-weary publics often appreciate parties that can credibly promise security and there is some survey evidence that exposure to protracted conflict leads a population to be more willing to accept authoritarian leaders.[46] Rebel movements often highlight the sacrifices made during the armed struggle and the valour of their martyrs. Victors do not need to rely upon winning credible post-conflict elections to claim legitimacy. Rebel tanks on the streets of the capitol provide ample evidence of the effective transfer of power. Some in a population may enthusiastically support the new order while others may resent it but it is difficult to deny the reality of a military victory.

Rebel winners of protracted civil war often claim to create a new political order rather than the more limited change of top-level leadership. In this way the rebel movements in Uganda, Ethiopia, and Rwanda share key characteristics with national liberation movements such as the Zimbabwe People's National Union, the South West African People's Organization (SWAPO), and the African National Congress. As Southall argues, these movements "could claim the authority of history, they and their leaders were imbued with a particular legitimacy, and challenges to their rule were therefore morally and politically illegitimate".[47] During the armed struggle, insurgents such as the NRA, TPLF, and RPF assert that they represent the "people" and have

FROM BULLETS TO BALLOTS

the right to rule because of the organization's commitment to needed social and political transformation. In Namibia, the victorious liberation movement transformed into the ruling party and used the campaign slogan "SWAPO is the nation and the nation is SWAPO".[48] Such narratives challenge the legitimacy of political competition and underline post-liberation parties' ambivalence if not hostility towards democracy.

Victorious insurgents must transform from organizations that developed in the context of wartime into organizations that can respond effectively to the different challenges of peace. As noted above, civil wars are not periods of anarchy or political vacuum but are alternative systems of governance based on fear and predation and that reward violence. If the insurgents remain unreconstructed, then the post-war regime is likely to be fragile. In Uganda, Ethiopia, and Rwanda, the creation of a strong authoritarian party was a key stage in the process of consolidating power and making the transition from victorious insurgent force to powerful and stable regime.

A significant challenge faced by the NRA, EPRDF, and RPF upon seizing power was that key national constituencies played minor roles in their respective insurgent movements. The popular bases of the three insurgencies were, to varying degrees, regionally and ethnically focused in contrast to the broader and more diverse bases needed to rule their respective post-conflict states. Civil wars are often fought in confined territories, as in the Luweero Triangle or Tigray, requiring victorious insurgent groups to reach out to populations outside of these zones as post-war parties in order to extend their authority throughout the state. Insurgent movements transform into political parties because such parties serve to broaden the base of the movement and make it a more effective organization to govern nationally post-war.

In Ethiopia, for example, the war was fought by the TPLF in the north and significant communities in the south had little contact with the insurgents prior to regime change. Populations from the historically marginalized Oromo and southern communities had been drafted into the Derg's army but most wished to stay out of the war. In 1989, the TPLF joined with a largely Amhara organization, the Ethiopian People's Democratic Movement, to form the coalition the EPRDF.[49] The EPRDF recognized this challenge and recruited leaders from among prisoners of war to form ethnic vanguards, to move quickly into southern areas after victory. These cadres established "peace and stability committees" within days of the regime change in 1991 and transformed these committees into political parties often known as "People's Democratic Organizations" throughout southern Ethiopia in time to dominate local elections in 1992.[50] These parties often were created virtually overnight and many had tenuous links to the often quite isolated communities in question.[51] By transforming the regionally and ethnically based insurgent movement into a national political party, the EPRDF had the kind of organizational capacity to extend its power into vast new areas for the first time.

Similarly in Uganda, leaders from the southern Ankole people and fighters from the Buganda dominated the NRM during the war. After victory, the movement deliberately reached out to old politicians from the Democratic Party to broaden its reach and to more closely resemble the ethnic complexity of Uganda.[52] The Tutsi-dominated RPF initially reached out to "moderate Hutus" so that it could position itself as a national party. By creating state-wide political parties, rebel movements with specific regional and ethnic origins could create new institutions that could claim to represent all of the population.

Elections and post-insurgent authoritarian parties

Post-conflict elections following rebel victory have little to do with determining who will govern but are often key processes for the transformation of rebel movements into national authoritarian parties. Uganda, Ethiopia, and Rwanda each held multiple rounds of post-conflict elections but these polls served to consolidate the authority of the victorious rebel group rather than being a mechanism for citizen participation. Beyond their consequences for legitimacy, electoral processes following civil war play other key functions that assist victorious rebels to demonstrate their domination, consolidate power, and engage in political party expansion.

Elections following rebel victory are typically non-competitive and function as processes of power consolidation rather than citizen participation in selecting their leaders. In Uganda, Ethiopia, and Rwanda the incumbents have all won by overwhelming majorities. In the 2010 elections in Ethiopia, the ruling party won 96.6% of the seats in the national parliament and in 2015 increased its share to 100%.[53] Rwandan President Paul Kagame, when asked if his 93% landslide in the 2010 election represented the will of the people, answered: "So, 93% – I wonder why it wasn't higher than that?"[54] Successful rebel groups are not constructed to win "50% + 1" shares of battles and post-insurgent political parties tend to see losing a constituency as similar to losing a battle. The point of elections organized by strong authoritarian parties is to demonstrate overwhelming, unassailable strength, not to create a governing coalition or to solicit the views of citizens.

Elections under powerful post-insurgent authoritarian regimes follow patterns similar to polls in electoral or competitive authoritarian systems.[55] Turnout is often high despite the lack of competition. Many voters, however, go to the polls in order to avoid being characterized as an opponent of the military regime. Voter turnout in Rwanda was 97% in 2003 and 98% in 2010.[56] In Ethiopia, voter turnout was 94% in 1995, 90% in 2000, 83% in the competitive 2005 elections, and 93% in 2010 and 2015.[57] Museveni regarded political parties as one of the instigators of internal strife and consequently banned political parties until 2005. Only the NRM was allowed to operate in the "no-party" system. In fact, as documented by Carbone, the NRM assumed many of the functions of a political party and handily won the first multi-party elections.[58] In 2016, just before the February election, an observer wrote:

> There are no prizes for predicting who wins Uganda's presidential election on 18 February. After 30 years in office and four victorious elections in the last 20 of them, President Yoweri Kaguta Museveni knows every trick in the book. Yet he's still taking no chances. Using state funds, intimidating and outlawing the opposition, and mobilizing violent "youth" are all part of the presidential armory. All this comes on top of his National Resistance Movement (NRM)'s overwhelming control of the electoral process and its unparalleled ability to mobilize the grassroots.[59]

Some voters explain that voting in non-competitive elections is a necessary task to avoid trouble with the powerful authoritarian party. As one Ethiopian farmer explained his 1995 vote for the ruling party, "I was afraid. The Government said I should vote so I voted. What could I do?"[60] Frightened voters can acquiesce to but not legitimate the power of strong authoritarian regimes. Elections following rebel victory provide opportunities for the authoritarian party to demonstrate its power and to marginalize potential rivals, both within the ruling party and from other potential sources of opposition. A victory of over 90% sends a powerful message that the ex-insurgent party remains over-whelmingly dominant and that compliance or acquiescence is necessary.

Conclusions

This article has identified mechanisms that show how victorious insurgent groups may transform into powerful post-war authoritarian political parties. One mechanism is the organizational legacies of wartime that shape the development patterns of post-war ruling parties. To engage in protracted armed conflict and to be viable as an actor in wartime governance requires an organization that operates in some ways as a proto-authoritarian party. Legacies of the protracted war – notably coherent and disciplined leadership, effective hierarchical links between leaders and rank-and-file, and experi-ence in mobilizing civilians in liberated territory – create models and precedents that provide a mechanism that links wartime rebel organizations to peacetime political parties.

A second set of mechanisms is connected to the process of the war-to-peace tran-sition following rebel victory. In contrast to cases of negotiated settlement and the liberal peace model supported by the international community with its emphasis on powersharing, third-party security guarantees, and building democratic institutions, the victorious insurgents dominate the transition following the defeat of the incumbent regime. Post-conflict elections and political parties are not just deployed by the inter-national community in cases of negotiated settlement but also help consolidate power and build authoritarianism following insurgent victory.

This article focused on Uganda, Ethiopia, and Rwanda, three cases where victorious insurgents transformed into authoritarian parties. To answer the larger question of how wartime institutions shape post-conflict politics requires an analysis of a broader range of cases of civil wars that ended in victory. Other cases are characterized by the rapid collapse of the old regime, in part due to significant external intervention from neigh-bours or the international community, as in the Democratic Republic of Congo in 1996 or Libya in 2011. Laurent-Désiré Kabila's Alliance of Democratic Forces for the Liber-ation of Congo-Zaire, for example, was a quickly assembled amalgamation of armed factions organized with significant assistance from neighbouring Uganda and Rwanda, rather than an insurgency with a battle-hardened leadership and experience in administering liberated territory.[61] In Libya, an international air campaign contrib-uted to the rapid collapse of Muammar Gaddafi's rule and the emergence of a patch-work of decentralized "revolutionary brigades".[62] In neither case did the insurgents have the time or incentives to forge the kind of strong institutional basis for an effective authoritarian ruling party.

There are other cases of insurgent victories that ended in self-determination, such as Namibia, Eritrea, and South Sudan.[63] These transitions raise different dynamics for vic-torious rebels compared to the challenges of consolidating power in existing states.[64] The old regime is no longer a political player in cases of secession. Finally, there are cases of civil wars that end with the victory of the incumbent state. The war-to-peace transitions in cases of government victory such as Algeria, Angola, Peru, Sri Lanka, and Russia (Chechnya) also differ from the East African cases examined here.

The three powerful authoritarian regimes with their origins in victorious insurgent groups under examination here – the NRM in Uganda, the EPRDF in Ethiopia, and the RPF in Rwanda – have remained in power since winning their respective wars. There

FROM BULLETS TO BALLOTS

are questions, however, regarding whether such parties have the flexibility to facilitate a transition from post-war authoritarian to a more sustainable democratic political order. The original leaders in Uganda and Rwanda remain in power in 2016 and are likely to retain their positions in upcoming elections. Meles Zenawi, the founder of the insurgent group that became the ruling party in Ethiopia, died in office in 2012 and was replaced by the deputy prime minister without any public drama, suggesting the resilience and continued relevance of the party beyond its founder. The legacies of victory, however, change over time. Cohesive leadership forged on the battlefield fades as new interests and actors emerge in peacetime. The legitimacy achieved through victory lessens in countries where the majority of the population has no direct memory of the war. The hierarchy and discipline that was associated with winning the war may create a ruling party that is powerful but also brittle.

Acronyms

EPRDF	Ethiopian People's Revolutionary Democratic Front
MLLT	Marxist-Leninist League of Tigray
NRA	National Resistance Army (Uganda)
NRM	National Resistance Movement (Uganda)
RC	Resistance Council
RPF	Rwandan Patriotic Front
SWAPO	South West African People's Organization
TPLF	Tigray People's Liberation Front

Disclosure statement

No potential conflict of interest was reported by the author.

Notes

1. LeBas, *From Protest to Parties*; Elischer, *Political Parties in Africa*.
2. Huntington, *Political Order in Changing Societies*, 424.
3. Michels, *Political Parties*, 367.
4. Manning, *The Politics of Peace in Mozambique*.
5. Ishiyama and Batta, "Swords into Plowshares."
6. Lyons, *Demilitarizing Politics*. See also Kovacs, *From Rebellion to Politics*; De Zeeuw, *From Soldiers to Politicians*.
7. Paris, *At War's End*. For a recent review of the concept see Richmond and Mac Ginty, "Where Now for the Critique of Liberal Peacebuilding?"
8. Tilly, "War Making and State Making"; Toft, *Securing the Peace*, 60.
9. Weinstein, *Inside Rebellion*.
10. Fortna and Huang, "Democratization after Civil War," 805.
11. Levitsky and Way, *Competitive Authoritarianism*.
12. See also Brownlee, *Authoritarianism in an Age of Democratization*; Gandhi, *Political Institutions under Dictatorship*; and Magaloni, *Voting for Autocracy*.
13. Geddes, "Authoritarian Breakdown."
14. Collier et al., *Breaking the Conflict Trap*, 56.
15. Southall, *Liberation Movements in Power*, 56–57.
16. Menkhaus, "Governance without Government."
17. Keen, "Incentives and Disincentives for Violence"; Duffield, *Global Governance and the New Wars*.
18. Staniland, "States, Insurgents, and Wartime Political Orders." See also Arjona, "Wartime Institutions"; Mampilly, *Rebel Rulers*.

FROM BULLETS TO BALLOTS

19. Della Porta, *Clandestine Political Violence*.
20. Collier, Hoeffler, and Rohner, "Beyond Greed and Grievance."
21. Downs, *An Economic Theory of Democracy*, 25.
22. Weinstein, *Inside Rebellion*; Wood, *Insurgent Collective Action*.
23. Christia, *Alliance Formation in Civil Wars*; Woldemariam, *When Rebels Collide*.
24. Herbst, "African Militaries and Rebellion." On the NRM see Museveni, *Sowing the Mustard Seed*, 7. On the TPLF see Young, *Peasant Revolution in Ethiopia*, 101–103. On the RPF see Misser, *Vers un Nouveau Rwanda?*
25. Ngoga, "Uganda," 100.
26. Ofcansky, *Uganda*.
27. Schubert, "'Guerillas Don't Die Easily.'"
28. Young, *Peasant Revolution in Ethiopia*; Hammond, *Fire from the Ashes*.
29. Milkias, "Ethiopia, the TPLF, and the Roots of the 2001 Political Tremor," 13.
30. Tronvoll, *War and the Politics of Identity in Ethiopia*, 49, 56.
31. Reed, "Exile, Reform, and the Rise of the Rwandan Patriotic Front."
32. Balcells and Kalyvas, "Does Warfare Matter?," 1395. See also Kalyvas and Balcells, "How the End of the Cold War Shaped Internal Conflict." For a case study see Daly, "Organizational Legacies of Violence."
33. Arjona, "Wartime Institutions."
34. Kasfir, "Guerrillas and Civilian Participation," 291.
35. Eriya Kategaya, a member of the NRA, quoted in Tideman, "Resistance Councils in Uganda," 82.
36. Cited in Tideman, "Resistance Councils in Uganda," 63.
37. Hammond, "Garrison Towns and the Control of Space in Revolutionary Tigray," 92–93.
38. Bach, "Abyotawi Democracy"; Lenin, *What is to be Done?*
39. Vaughan and Tronvoll, *The Culture of Power in Contemporary Ethiopian Political Life*.
40. Berhe, *A Political History of the Tigray People's Liberation Front*, 252.
41. Africa Watch, *Evil Days*, 309; Barnabas and Zwi, "Health Policy Development in Wartime," 42.
42. Hendrie, "The Politics of Repatriation."
43. Prendergast and Duffield, *Without Troops and Tanks*.
44. Watson, *Exile from Rwanda*.
45. Muhanguzi, "Visiting RPA's Captured Territory."
46. Dyrstad, "Does Civil War Breed Authoritarian Values?"
47. Southall, *Liberation Movements in Power*, 6.
48. See Melber, "Limits to Liberation."
49. The EPDM later recast itself as the Amhara National Democratic Movement.
50. Vaughan and Tronvoll, *The Culture of Power in Contemporary Ethiopian Political Life*, 116.
51. For the example of the Omotic People's Democratic Front, see Markakis, *Ethiopia: The Last Two Frontiers*, 337.
52. Tripp, *Museveni's Uganda*, 48–49. See also Lindemann, "Just Another Change of the Guard?"
53. Arriola and Lyons, "Ethiopia."
54. AFP, "Rwandan President."
55. Schedler, *Electoral Authoritarianism*.
56. Reyntjens, "Rwanda."
57. Voter turnout data from International IDEA available at http://www.idea.int/vt/countryview. cfm?id=73. The figures for Uganda are not as dramatic – 59% in 1996, 70% in 2001, 68% in 2006, and 59% in 2011.
58. Carbone, *No-Party Democracy?*
59. Africa Confidential, "Uganda."
60. Quoted in Buckley, "Ethiopia Takes New Ethnic Tack," A21.
61. Stearns, *Dancing in the Glory of Monsters*.
62. International Crisis Group, *Popular Protest in North Africa and the Middle East*.
63. Somaliland is a similar case, but has not been recognized as a new state by the international community.
64. For a discussion see Toft, "Self-Determination, Secession, and Civil War."

Bibliography

AFP. "Rwandan President: 93 Percent of the Vote Was Not Enough." June 7, 2011, available at http://www.rnw.nl/africa/bulletin/rwandan-president-93-vote-was-not-enough (accessed October 10, 2014).

Africa Watch. *Evil Days: 30 Years of War and Famine in Ethiopia.* New York: Africa Watch, Spring, 1991.

Arjona, A. "Wartime Institutions: A Research Agenda." *Journal of Conflict Resolution* 58, no. 8 (2014): 1360–1389.

Arriola, L. R., and T. Lyons. "Ethiopia: The 100% Election." *Journal of Democracy* 27, no 1 (2016): 76–88.

Bach, J.-N. "Abyotawi Democracy: Neither Revolutionary nor Democratic, a Critical View of EPRDF's Conception of Revolutionary Democracy in post-1991 Ethiopia." *Journal of Eastern African Studies* 5 no. 4 (2011): 641–663.

Balcells, L., and S. N. Kalyvas. "Does Warfare Matter? Security, Duration, and Outcomes of Civil War." *Journal of Conflict Resolution* 58, no. 8 (2014): 1390–1418.

Barnabas, G., and A. Zwi. "Health Policy Development in Wartime: Establishing the Baito Health Care System in Tigray, Ethiopia." *Health Policy and Planning* 12, no. 1 (1997): 38–49.

Berhe, Aregawi. *A Political History of the Tigray People's Liberation Front (1975–1991): Revolt, Ideology and Mobilisation in Ethiopia.* Los Angeles, CA: Teshai Press, 2009.

Brownlee, J. *Authoritarianism in an Age of Democratization.* Cambridge: Cambridge University Press, 2007.

Buckley, S. "Ethiopia Takes New Ethnic Tack: Deliberately Divisive." *The Washington Post* June 18, 1995, p. A21.

Carbone, Giovanni. *No-Party Democracy? Ugandan Politics in Comparative Perspective.* Boulder, CO: Lynne Rienner Publishers, 2008.

Christia, F. *Alliance Formation in Civil Wars.* Cambridge: Cambridge University Press, 2012.

Collier, P., V. L. Elliott, H. Hegre, A. Hoeffler, M. Reynal-Querol, and N. Sambanis. *Breaking the Conflict Trap: Civil War and Development Policy.* Washington, DC: World Bank Policy Research Report, 2003.

Collier, P., A. Hoeffler, and D. Rohner. "Beyond Greed and Grievance: Feasibility and Civil War." *Oxford Economic Papers* 61 (2009): 1–27.

Daly, S. Z. "Organizational Legacies of Violence: Conditions Favoring Insurgency Onset in Colombia, 1964–1984." *Journal of Peace Research* 49, no. 3 (May 2012): 473–491.

De Zeeuw, J., ed. *From Soldiers to Politicians: Transforming Rebel Movements after Civil War.* Boulder, CO: Lynne Rienner, 2007.

Della Porta, D. *Clandestine Political Violence.* Cambridge: Cambridge University Press, 2013.

Downs, A. *An Economic Theory of Democracy.* Boston, MA: Addison Wesley, 1957.

Duffield, M. *Global Governance and the New Wars: The Merging of Development and Security.* London: Zed, 2001.

Dyrstad, K. "Does Civil War Breed Authoritarian Values? An Empirical Study of Bosnia-Herzegovina, Kosovo, and Croatia." *Democratization* 20, no. 7 (July 2012): 1219–1242.

Elischer, S. *Political Parties in Africa: Ethnicity and Party Formation.* Cambridge: Cambridge University Press, 2013.

Fortna, V. P., and R. Huang. "Democratization after Civil War: A Brush-Clearing Exercise." *International Studies Quarterly* 56, no. 4 (December 2012): 801–808.

Gandhi, J. *Political Institutions under Dictatorship*. Cambridge: Cambridge University Press, 2008.

Geddes, B. "Authoritarian Breakdown: Empirical Test of a Game Theoretic Argument." Paper presented at the American Political Science Association Meetings, 1999.

Hammond, J. "Garrison Towns and the Control of Space in Revolutionary Tigray." In *Remapping Ethiopia: Socialism and After*, edited by W. James, E. Kurimoto, D. Donham, and A. Triuzi. London: James Currey, 2002, 90–108.

Hammond, J. *Fire from the Ashes: A Chronicle of the Revolution in Tigray, Ethiopia*. Lawrenceville, NJ: Red Sea Press, 1999.

Hendrie, B. "The Politics of Repatriation: The Tigrayan Refugee Repatriation 1985–1987." *Journal of Refugee Studies* 4, no. 2 (June 1991): 200–218.

Herbst, J. "African Militaries and Rebellion: The Political Economy of Threat and Combat Effectiveness." *Journal of Peace Research* 41, no. 3 (May 2004): 357–369.

Huntington, S. *Political Order in Changing Societies*. New Haven, CT: Yale University Press, 1968.

International Crisis Group. *Popular Protest in North Africa and the Middle East (V)*: Making Sense of Libya. Middle East/North Africa Report no. 107, 6 June 2011.

Ishiyama, J., and A. Batta. "Swords into Plowshares: The Organizational Transformation of Rebel Groups into Political Parties." *Communist and Post-Communist Studies* 44, no. 4 (December 2011): 369–379.

Kalyvas, S. N., and L. Balcells. "International System and Technologies of Rebellion: How the End of the Cold War Shaped Internal Conflict." *American Political Science Review* 104, no. 3 (2010): 415–429.

Kasfir, N. "Guerrillas and Civilian Participation: The National Resistance Army in Uganda, 1981–86." *Journal of Modern African Studies* 43, no. 2 (June 2005): 271–296.

Keen, David. "Incentives and Disincentives for Violence." In *Greed and Grievance: Economic Agendas in Civil Wars*, edited by Mats Berdal and David Malone. Boulder, CO: Lynne Rienner, 2000, 19–42.

Kovacs, M. S. *From Rebellion to Politics. The Transformation of Rebel Groups to Political Parties in Civil War Peace Processes*. Uppsala: Department of Peace and Conflict Research, Uppsala University, 2007.

LeBas, A. *From Protest to Parties: Party Building and Democratization in Africa*. Oxford: Oxford University Press, 2011.

Lenin, V. *What is to be Done?* 1902. https://www.marxists.org/archive/lenin/works/1901/witbd/ch03.htm.

Levitsky, S., and L. Way. *Competitive Authoritarianism: Hybrid Regimes After the Cold War*. Cambridge: Cambridge University Press, 2010.

Lindemann, S. "Just Another Change of the Guard? Broad-Based Politics and Civil War in Museveni's Uganda." *African Affairs* 110, no. 440 (July 2011): 387–416.

Lyons, T. *Demilitarizing Politics: Elections on the Uncertain Road to Peace*. Boulder, CO: Lynne Rienner, 2005.

Magaloni, B. *Voting for Autocracy: Hegemonic Party Survival and Its Demise in Mexico*. Cambridge: Cambridge University Press, 2006.

Mampilly, Z. C. *Rebel Rulers: Insurgent Governance and Civilian Life During War*. Ithaca, NY: Cornell University Press, 2011.

Manning, C. *The Politics of Peace in Mozambique: Post-Conflict Democratization, 1992–2000*. New York: Praeger, 2002.

Markakis, J. *Ethiopia: The Last Two Frontiers*. New York: James Currey, 2011.

Melber, H. "Limits to Liberation: An Introduction to Namibia's Post-colonial Political Culture." In *Re-examining Liberation in Namibia: Political Culture since Independence*, edited by H. Melber. Uppsala: Nordic African Institute, 2003, 9–24

Menkhaus, K. "Governance without Government in Somalia: Spoilers, State Building, and the Politics of Coping." *International Security* 31, no. 3 (2006/07): 74–106.

Michels, R. *Political Parties: A Sociological Study of the Oligarchical Tendencies of Modern Democracy*. New York: Free Press, 1962.

Milkias. "Ethiopia, the TPLF, and the Roots of the 2001 Political Tremor." *Northeast African Studies* 10, no. 2 (2003): 13–66.

Misser, F. *Vers un Nouveau Rwanda? Entretiens avec Paul Kagame*. Paris: Karthala, 1995.

Muhanguzi, J. "Visiting RPA's Captured Territory." *The Observer*, November 23, 2015. http://observer.ug/special-editions/41188-visiting-rpa-s-captured-territory.

FROM BULLETS TO BALLOTS

Museveni, Y. *Sowing the Mustard Seed: The Struggle for Freedom and Democracy in Uganda*. London: Macmillan, 1986.

Ngoga, P. "Uganda: The National Resistance Army." In *African Guerillas*, edited by C. Clapham. James Currey, 1998, 91–106.

Ofcansky, T. *Uganda: Tarnished Pearl of Africa*. Boulder, CO: Westview, 1999.

Paris, R. *At War's End*. Cambridge: Cambridge University Press, 2004.

Prendergast, J., and M. Duffield. *Without Troops and Tanks: The Emergency Relief Desk and the Cross Border Operation in Eritrea and Tigray*. Trenton, NJ: Red Sea Press, 1994.

Reed, W. C. "Exile, Reform, and the Rise of the Rwandan Patriotic Front." *Journal of Modern African Studies* 34, no. 3 (September 1996): 479–501.

Reyntjens, Filip. "Rwanda: Progress of Powder Keg?" *Journal of Democracy* 26, no. 3 (July 2015): 19–33.

Richmond, O. P., and R. Mac Ginty. "Where Now for the Critique of Liberal Peacebuilding?" *Cooperation and Conflict* 50, no. 2 (June 2015): 171–189.

Schedler, A. *Electoral Authoritarianism: The Dynamics of Unfree Competition*. Boulder, Colo: Lynne Rienner, 2006.

Schubert, F. "'Guerillas Don't Die Easily': Everyday Life in Wartime and the Guerrilla Myth in the National Resistance Army in Uganda, 1981–1986." *International Review of Social History* 51, no. 1 (April 2006): 93–111.

Southall, R. *Liberation Movements in Power: Party and State in Southern Africa*. London: James Currey, 2013.

Staniland, P. "States, Insurgents, and Wartime Political Orders." *Perspectives on Politics* 10, no. 2 (June 2012): 243–264.

Stearns, J. *Dancing in the Glory of Monsters: The Collapse of Congo and the Great War of Africa*. New York: Public Affairs, 2011.

Tideman, P. "Resistance Councils in Uganda: A Study of Rural Politics and Popular Democracy in Africa." PhD diss., Roskilde University, Denmark, 1994.

Tilly, C. "War Making and State Making as Organized Crime." In *Bringing the State Back In*, edited by P. Evans, D. Rueschemeyer, and T. Skocpol. Cambridge: Cambridge University Press, 1985, 169–191.

Toft, M. D. "Self-Determination, Secession, and Civil War." *Terrorism and Political Violence* 24 (2012): 581–600.

Toft, M. D. *Securing the Peace: The Durable Settlement of Civil War*. Princeton, NJ: Princeton University Press, 2010.

Tripp, A. M. *Museveni's Uganda: Paradoxes of Power in a Hybrid Regime*. Boulder, CO: Lynne Rienner Publishers, 2010.

Tronvoll, K. *War and the Politics of Identity in Ethiopia: Making Enemies and Allies in the Horn of Africa*. London: James Currey, 2009.

"Uganda: How the Next Election Will be Won." *Africa Confidential* 57, no. 30 (5 February 2016): 1–2.

Vaughan, S., and K. Tronvoll. *The Culture of Power in Contemporary Ethiopian Political Life*. Stockholm: SIDA Study no. 10, 2003.

Watson, C. *Exile from Rwanda: Background to an Invasion*. Washington, DC: US Committee for Refugees, 1991.

Weinstein, J. M. *Inside Rebellion: The Politics of Insurgent Violence*. Cambridge: Cambridge University Press, 2007.

Woldemariam, Michael H. "When Rebels Collide: Factionalism and Fragmentation in African Insurgencies." (PhD diss., Princeton University, 2011).

Wood, E. J. *Insurgent Collective Action and Civil War in El Salvador*. Cambridge: Cambridge University Press, 2003.

Young, J. *Peasant Revolution in Ethiopia: The Tigray People's Liberation Front, 1975–1991*. New York: Cambridge University Press, 1997.

RESEARCH ARTICLE

The Guatemalan National Revolutionary unit: the long collapse

Michael E. Allison

Department of Political Science, University of Scranton, Scranton, PA, USA

ABSTRACT
The Guatemalan National Revolutionary Unit (URNG) fought one of the longest and bloodiest civil wars in recent Latin American history. In 1996, the URNG and the Government of Guatemala signed a Firm and Lasting Agreement ending the country's civil war and initiating the URNG's post-war life as a political party. After finishing third in its initial electoral competition, the URNG has since been unable to capture more than 4% of the vote, on its own or in coalition, leaving it a minor political party. What explains the poor electoral performance of the URNG as a political party? Based upon fieldwork, elite interviews, and analysis of electoral data, I argue that the URNG's minor party performance was caused by both organizational and institutional factors.

Several former rebel groups have successfully made the transition to political party and researchers recently have begun to ask why some have succeeded while others have not.[1] In Latin America, some groups, such as the Farabundo Martí National Liberation Front (FMLN) in El Salvador, made the transition following negotiated settlements to civil wars. Others, such as the Sandinista National Liberation Front (FSLN) in Nicaragua, did so after having emerged militarily victorious.[2] Finally, other rebel groups, such as the Tupamaros in Uruguay, transitioned to political parties after having been defeated.[3] What is interesting here is that these three rebel groups eventually won political power through the democratic process even though each war had a different outcome. But most rebel groups turned political parties are not nearly as successful as the Sandinistas, FMLN, and Tupamaros. And while it is surely important to know why these groups succeeded as political parties, as many have attempted to do, it is equally important to understand why other groups have not experienced similar success.

After several years of operating independently, the Rebel Armed Forces (FAR), Organization of the People in Arms (ORPA), Guerrilla Army of the Poor (EGP) and Guatemalan Workers' Party (PGT) formed the Guatemalan National Revolutionary

Unit (URNG) in February 1982. For the next 14 years, the Marxist-Leninist URNG battled the country's armed forces in what was one of the longest and bloodiest civil wars in recent Latin American history, leaving an estimated mostly indigenous 200,000–250,000 killed or disappeared and another two million displaced. Although the conflict clearly had indigenous dimensions, the URNG sought revolutionary change that would replace an authoritarian regime that had been imposed following a 1954 CIA-orchestrated coup that removed a progressive government with a socialist-oriented political and economic system. After a decade-long peace process, the URNG and President Alvaro Arzú signed the Firm and Lasting Agreement in December 1996. After competing in four national elections since the war's conclusion, the URNG remains a marginal force in Guatemalan politics.

Why did one of the region's longest-surviving rebel groups perform so poorly as a political party? On the following pages, I discuss how a rebel group's background might prove useful when it undertakes a transition to political party and how the political environment into which a former rebel group integrates might affect its performance. Based upon fieldwork in 2004, 2010 and 2013, two dozen elite interviews, and an analysis of electoral data, I argue that the URNG has fared poorly because of both organizational (minimal combatants and noncombatants, internal divisions, a strained relationship with civil society, and the lack of a political wing) and institutional (relatively unfavourable electoral rules) factors.

Organizational and institutional challenges

It is clear that civil war outcome is not the only factor likely to explain the performance of former rebel groups as political parties. As rebels, these groups varied with regard to the national territory that they controlled, contacts with nonviolent organizations, and combatants under their command. While these differences most likely contributed to their war-time performances, it is also likely that they contributed to their performances as political parties as well. New political parties require the support of a number of full- and part-time staff to mount an effective campaign, including collecting signatures, distributing campaign materials, and volunteering at the polls. Some rebel groups command hundreds of armed combatants while others might count on the support of tens of thousands. One can look at the small but successful revolutionary movements in Cuba and Nicaragua relative to the comparatively larger and better equipped, yet less successful, revolutionary movements in Colombia and El Salvador. While large numbers of rebel forces are not necessarily essential for military success, it would seem likely that larger groups preparing for electoral competition would be better positioned than smaller groups.

Another issue likely to affect the electoral performance of these new political parties pertains to whether a rebel group establishes a political wing during a conflict.[4] First, we can imagine that a revolutionary group might create a political wing to disseminate propaganda and to publicize collective grievances and the goals of the organization to both domestic and international audiences. This might contribute to its favourable perception not only during the war but in the post-war period. Second, the existence of a political wing might further help the group if it actually competes in the electoral process while the rebel group continues fighting. For example, the Salvadoran Democratic Revolutionary Front (FDR) helped to promote the FMLN both within the country and abroad before competing in the 1989 elections as the Democratic Convergence

FROM BULLETS TO BALLOTS

and, once in congress, helping to smooth the FMLN's transition to political party. The experience that a political wing gains by competing in elections and the voter loyalties it cultivates might contribute to the future success of the new political party.

Likewise, some rebel groups develop extensive ties to mass-based organizations (unions, student organizations, and peasant confederations), while other groups are unable or unwilling to cultivate relations with broader sectors of civil society.[5] Rebel and mass-based groups can coordinate opposition to the regime through simultaneous work stoppages, national strikes, civil disobedience, and guerrilla attacks. The development of a broad-based opposition coalition has been found to be a key determinant of revolutionary success.[6] Even if a strong relationship with mass-based organizations does not lead to military victory, it might prove helpful at forging a negotiated settlement.[7] We would also expect the development of a broad-based coalition to contribute to the success of the new political party as it will provide the party with a pool of potential voters and committed party activists.

Another concern relevant to former rebel groups relates to organizational unity. Rebel coalitions can fracture in the midst of war, negotiations, and the post-war period. Differences over strategies and tactics can lead to intra-group conflict that might undermine the attainment of the group's military goals. On the other hand, rebel groups might not suffer from problems of incoherence during the war when they all share the belief in the military defeat of the government, but instead when the rebels contemplate a shift to nonviolent tactics.[8] As a result, the new parties might lose key leaders and individuals sympathetic to the party as well as voters. Therefore, groups that can avoid disintegrating or fragmenting should be more successful than those that succumb to these forces.[9]

While focusing solely upon the characteristics of former insurgent groups can go a long way towards explaining their electoral performance, explaining their success or failure would be incomplete without considering the institutional environment in which the groups must compete.[10] Environments may be more or less conducive to facilitating new party success. Because the URNG competes in a presidential system, I focus here on basic differences within presidential systems that might impact a new party's performance.

One important way in which presidential systems differ relates to the rules utilized to elect the president. Scholars have found that plurality voting tends to depress the number of parties whereas majority voting leads to greater multipartism.[11] In majority-vote systems, the opportunity for political parties to succeed will be enhanced by their ability to participate in a first round of voting and, given that the new political party is unlikely to attain a 50% majority in the first round, it can use its first round support to leverage concessions from one of the two larger parties prior to the second round of voting. This influence can then help the new party going forward.

New political parties are also more likely to succeed in electoral systems where members are elected by proportional representation (PR) rather than single member district (SMD) voting.[12] SMD voting tends to create a two-party system by over-representing the two largest parties, thus making it more difficult for new political parties to emerge and succeed. Both political leaders and voters are drawn to the two largest parties with the greatest chance of winning the seat, often hurting these former rebel parties. Political systems employing PR, on the other hand, tend to have the goal of preventing the over-representation and the under-representation of political parties. Therefore, former rebel groups are more likely to succeed as new political parties in those systems employing PR where the percentage of seats they capture in the legislature will closely approximate the percentage of votes they receive.[13] But most countries also tend to institute an electoral threshold to limit the proliferation of new political parties. Too many small political parties can make the policy-making process highly inefficient. Parties are thereby required to win a number of seats "in the lower-tier districts and/or a minimum percentage of the total national vote" to retain legal standing.[14] While high electoral thresholds should prevent a proliferation of new, small political parties, lower electoral thresholds should increase the average number of new political parties competing in the system. Former rebel groups confront many obstacles upon initial electoral competition, which makes it likely that electoral thresholds will impact their performance.

A marginal electoral force

There are several indicators through which we can assess the performance of new political parties. First, and at its most basic, we can determine whether the party simply persists by meeting the minimum requirements needed to remain officially recognized as a political party. While persistence might be a minimal condition of success, most political parties are likely to be severely disappointed if the best they can do is to simply surpass some minimal legal threshold. At the other end of the spectrum, winning the presidency would most likely be the ultimate prize as it is clearly the most important position. Considering that winning the presidency might be too much to ask of new parties, we might view a new political party that increases its vote totals over a series of elections as more successful than a new party that loses its electoral share over time.

When competitive elections returned to Guatemala in 1985, twelve political parties competed. All 12 have subsequently disappeared. At the same time, every presidential election has been won by a different political party. The fluid nature of the country's political system has led Sánchez to call it a "party nonsystem" "characterized by persistently high transfers of votes away from the main parties towards new and small parties (that is, high extrasystemic volatility), an ever-changing constellation of parties without a stable 'core'".[15] It is not just that today's winners are likely to be tomorrow's losers. Today's winners are likely to disappear and tomorrow's winners have yet to be established. Given this extreme volatility, the URNG now possesses one of the most extensive electoral histories of any current political party in Guatemala (Table 1).

The New Nation Alliance (ANN)/URNG's 1999 presidential candidate, Alvaro Colom Caballeros, finished third with 12% of the national vote. The Guatemalan constitution requires that the president be elected with a majority of the vote and since no candidate captured a majority of the vote, Alfonso Portillo of the Guatemalan Republican Front (FRG) defeated Oscar Berger of the National Advancement Party (PAN) 68% to 32% in a runoff. The fact that the URNG needed to compete in a coalition and that it captured only slightly more than 1 in 10 votes led many to declare the URNG's transition to political party dead on arrival. However, third place and 12% of the national vote should not have been too far off what was expected and, in retrospect, should have been celebrated. While most URNG and former URNG with whom I have spoken recognized that they finished far behind the first two political parties, they were nevertheless satisfied with their initial performance. In spite of all the challenges, the URNG's performance demonstrated that there was a bloc of voters willing to support it as a leftist alternative.

Table 1. Post-war presidential elections in Guatemala (votes and % of total votes).

Party	1999		2003		2007		2011	
	Round 1	Round 2	Round 1	Round 2	Round 1	Round 2	Round 1	Round 2
FRG	1,045,820 (48%)	1,173,823 (68%)	518,328 (19%)		239,208 (7%)		122,800 (3%)	
PAN	664,417 (30%)	545,151 (32%)	224,127 (8%)		83,826 (3%)			
URNG	**270,891 (12%)**[a]		**69,297 (3%)**		**70,080 (2%)**		**145,080 (3%)**[b]	
DCG	–		42,186 (2%)		16,529 (1%)			
FDNG	28,108 (1%)		–		–			
UCN	22,939 (1%)				103,603 (3%)		387,001 (9%)	
GANA	–		921,233 (34%)	1,235,219 (54%)	565,270 (17%)			
UNE	–		707,578 (26%)	1,046,744 (46%)	926,244 (28%)	1,449,153 (53%)		
ANN			–		19,377 (1%)			
DIA	–		59,774 (2%)		18,819 (1%)			
PU	–		80,943 (3%)		95,743 (3%)		97,498 (2%)	
PP					771,175 (24%	1,294,645 (47%)	1,604,472 (36%)	2,300,998 (54%)
EG					101,316 (3%)		277,365 (6%)[c]	
LIDER			3,676,280				1,016,340 (23%)	1,981,048 (46%)
CREO							737,452 (17%)	
Other	159,337 (7%)		60,313 (2%)		269,419 (8%)		65,924 (2%)	
Valid Votes	2,191,512	1,718,974	2,683,779	2,281,963	3,280,609	2,743,798	4,453,932	4,282,046

[a]In 1999 the URNG competed at part of the ANN coalition in support of Alvaro Colom Caballeros.
[b]In 2011, the URNG competed as part of the Broad Front along with Winaq, ANN, and MNR.
[c]EG and ViVa supported Haroldo Caballeros.

FROM BULLETS TO BALLOTS

However, by the time of the 2003 elections, the URNG was in a much weaker position. It would never again regain the electoral support that it captured in its first contest. With former ORPA commander Rodrigo Asturias and EGP and indigenous leader Pablo Ceto as presidential and vice-presidential candidates, the URNG finished sixth with 3% of the vote. Oscar Berger (formerly of the PAN and second-place finisher in 1999) of the Grand National Alliance defeated Alvaro Colom (formerly of the ANN/URNG alliance) of the National Unity of Hope, 54% to 46%. Similarly to 1999, the URNG was unable to negotiate an alliance with either party that advanced to the second round even though Colom had previously represented their coalition.

In 2007, the URNG-MAIZ's Miguel Ángel Sandoval and Walda Barrios captured slightly more than 2% of the vote while the ex-guerrillas in the ANN, now a separate political party composed largely of former FAR militants, captured less than 1%. Finally, the centre-left alliance of Encounter for Guatemala-Winaq that supported Nobel laureate Rigoberta Menchú received 3.09% of the national vote. In November 2007, Colom defeated Otto Pérez Molina in a runoff 53% to 47%.

In 2011, the URNG joined with the New Nation Alternative (ANN), Winaq, New Republic Movement, and other leftist organizations to form the Broad Front of the Left.[16] However, several social organizations abandoned the Broad Front once Menchú was selected as the alliance's candidate. While the left demonstrated greater excitement in 2011, it once again captured a disappointing 3.26% of the vote. More than anything else, the Broad Front was an electoral alliance among elites at the national level with little buy-in at the departmental and municipal levels.[17]

The URNG's share of the presidential vote has declined from a high of 12% in coalition in 1999 to 2.58% in 2003 and then to a low of 2.14% in 2007. When the left worked together in 2011, its electoral support increased ever so slightly to 3.27%. In terms of the absolute vote, the URNG has also experienced a severe decline before reversing that trend in 2011. After capturing 270,891 votes in 1999, the URNG was only able to amass 69,297 votes in 2003 and 70,080 in 2007. However, it more than doubled its votes to 145,080 in 2011. The URNG has not succeeded in capturing the presidency in four attempts and has played little role in determining any outcomes (Table 2).

In order to persist, the URNG has had to win at least one congressional seat at the district level or to have surpassed a 4% (5% since 2004) threshold nationally. In 1999, the URNG easily cleared the 4% hurdle with 11% of the legislative vote as part of the ANN/URNG. The ANN/URNG captured nine seats (or 8% of the congress's 113 seats), two from the national list and seven from departmental lists (one for Guatemala City, and one each in the departments of Huehuetenango, Quiché, Alta Verapaz, San Marcos, Quetzaltenango, and Guatemala). However, only five seats accurately belonged to the URNG as four were maintained by their coalition partners.

Prior to the 2003 elections, the number of congressional seats available increased from 113 to 158. However, the URNG still came close to losing its legal standing when it received a shade over 4% of the departmental and national vote in capturing two seats, one from the national list and one from Huehuetenango. In 2007, now as the URNG-MAIZ, its vote share declined to 3.27% while capturing two seats, one again in Huehuetenango and one from the national list.

Finally in 2011, the URNG won three seats (two to the URNG and one to Menchú's Winaq) with 3.23% of the vote as part of the Broad Front of the Left along with a number of small leftist parties and social groups. The national list seat was won by Winaq and the San Marcos and Huehuetenango seats by the URNG. In percentage

Table 2. Post-war legislative elections in Guatemala.

Political Party	1999		2003		2007		2011	
	Votes (vote %)	Seats (seat %)	Votes (vote %)	Seats (seat %)	Votes (vote %)	Seats (seat %)	Votes (vote %)	Seats (seat %)
FRG	891,429 (42%)	63 (56%)	502,470 (20%)	43 (27%)	306,166 (10%)	17 (11%)	120,105 (3%)	1 (1%)
PAN	570,108 (27%)	37 (33%)	278,393 (11%)	17 (11%)	143,268 (5%)	3 (2%)	136,247 (3%)	2 (1%)
URNG	**233,870[a] (11%)**	**9 (8%)[a]**	**107,276 (4%)**	**2 (1%)**	**112,249 (4%)**	**2 (1%)**	**143,238 (3%)**	**2 (1%)[b]**
DCG	86,839 (4%)	2 (2%)	82,324 (3%)		25,450 (1%)			
FDNG	60,821 (3%)		—					
UCN	42,921 (2%)		—		128,109 (4%)	5 (3%)	418,175 (10%)	14 (9%)
UN	—		17,478 (1%)		44,359 (1%)	1 (1%)		
UD	—		55,793 (2%)	2 (1%)	720,285 (23%)	51 (32%)	985,610 (22%)	36 (23%)
UNE	—		457,308 (18%)	32 (20%)	192,295 (6%)	7 (4%)	118,309 (3%)	1 (1%)
PU	—		157,893 (6%)	7 (4%)	521,600 (17%)	37 (23%)		
GANA	—		620,121 (24%)	47 (30%)	43,148 (1%)	0		
ANN			123,853 (5%)	6 (4%)	493,791 (16%)	29 (18%)		
PP					194,809 (6%)	4 (3%)	1,165,221 (27%)	57 (36%)
EG							345,709 (8%)	3 (2%)
LIDER							387,378 (9%)	14 (9%)
CREO							382,730 (9%)	12 (8%)
Other	231,884 (11%)	2 (2%)	149,465 (6%)		230,687 (7%)	5 (3%)	182,735 (4%)	4 (3%)
Valid votes / seats	2,117,872	113	2,552,374	158	3,153,216	158	4,385,457	158

[a]The URNG won these seats as a member of the ANN in 1999. Five of the nine seats were occupied by URNG candidates while the other four were controlled by coalition partners.
[b]The URNG won two seats and Winaq one.

terms, however, the URNG did no better in 2011 than it had in 2007. The URNG's total vote declined from a high of 231,384 (1999) to 104,876 (2003) to 103,480 (2007) before rebounding to 143,238 (2011). Given the extreme volatility of Guatemala's political system since the return to electoral democracy in 1985, the URNG's persistence is more of an achievement than initially meets the eye. After 12 years of electoral competition, however, the URNG remains a minor party.

Weak organizational ties and disadvantageous electoral rules

After three-plus decades of war, including 14 as a coalition, why did the Guatemalan rebels perform so poorly as a political party? During its demobilization and transition to political party, the URNG "was revealed to have a relatively small organization and not one with a large group of cadres trained or prepared to be political or electoral organizers".[18] Guatemalan rebels were thought to have numbered 6000–7500, with self-reported guerrilla estimates closer to 15,000–20,000 around 1980.[19] The scorched-earth offensive carried out by the military against the civilian population killed over 100,000 Guatemalans between 1981 and 1983 alone, simultaneously dealing a deadly blow to the URNG. Many URNG members were killed, fled into exile, or decided instead to participate in a revitalized civil society.[20] These defections and deaths included many mid-level cadres, leaving the URNG as an organization of commanders and foot soldiers.

A UN peacekeeping force oversaw the demobilization and disarmament of 5753 URNG members, including 2940 armed combatants and 2813 international and political support members.[21] Many believe the demobilization process actually overestimated the URNG's true strength and that the more accurate number of combatants stood as low as 1000–1500, perhaps even 500, as many of the demobilized were children and elderly.[22] However, I have also been told that many militants did not participate in the demobilization process because of frustration with the process or out of fear. Even so, we are only referring to a few hundred additional combatants.

For comparisons sake, while both the Salvadoran FMLN and URNG were numerically smaller than at earlier points in their respective histories, the FMLN (15,009) still remained significantly larger than the URNG (5753) at the end of its war. In relative terms, the FMLN was more than four times larger than the URNG if we compare the number of rebels to the total population in each country. Using El Salvador's total population according to the 1992 census (5,118,599), the FMLN demobilized 293 members per 100,000 Salvadorans. The URNG, on the other hand, demobilized 69 militants for every 100,000 Guatemalans based upon the 1994 census (8,331,874). The FMLN captured 25% in its first election. Given that Guatemala's territory is much larger than that of El Salvador, the limited number of personnel made it even more difficult for the party to carry out political activities.

There is good reason to believe that the URNG was also hindered because of the backgrounds of its demobilized rebels. Former guerrilla Alberto Ramírez Recinos argued that many who joined the guerrillas in the latter years did so out of revenge and were not politically conscious like earlier recruits.[23] Others blamed the failure of the URNG's commanders to lead them in the post-war period. Wilson Romero, former guerrilla and current professor, argues that they "totally underestimated" the effort necessary to transform themselves into a political party and its leadership "never had any experiences with the traditional Guatemalan political system".[24]

Arnoldo Villagrán, Rodrigo Asturias and Miguel Angel Albizures also lamented the lack of knowledge in building a political party and running an electoral campaign.[25]

The URNG might have been able to overcome its unfamiliarity with electoral politics had it established strong relations with those who did. The rebels attempted to create political organizations during the 1970s, but government repression and an inability to coordinate goals and tactics with these organizations led to their destruction.[26] When in January 1982 the URNG issued a public pronouncement of its revolutionary platform, the proclamation fell on deaf ears as the URNG lacked the political wing to publicize it – a noted contrast from the ties between the FMLN and the FDR.[27]

It was not until the mid-1990s that what could be more accurately, but not entirely, interpreted as a political wing was established. In 1994, the URNG encouraged the formation of the New Guatemala Democratic Front (FDNG). However, not all members of the FDNG were overly supportive of the insurgents[28] as a division existed between the democratic (those connected to human-rights organizations and a variety of social movements) and revolutionary left (those closely aligned with the revolutionary platform of the guerrillas). The FDNG's successful performance in 1995 convinced the URNG leadership that they had a future as a political party.[29] However, any experience with the electoral process was lost when relations between the URNG and FDNG collapsed prior to the 1999 elections.

Following its demobilization, the URNG made it clear that it did not want to integrate into the FDNG since that organization did not share its revolutionary ideals; nor did the FDNG desire to integrate into the URNG. However, they were both open to some sort of electoral alliance as some FDNG members had previously been involved in the guerrillas and the URNG realized that it was a relatively small organization wholly unprepared for the demands of party politics.[30] The left, albeit temporarily, formed a broad coalition to compete in the 1999 elections involving the URNG, FDNG, and other progressive groups. But the FDNG did not see the coalition as one built on mutual respect and did not believe that the URNG was interested in selecting candidates who might be considered "qualified" for elective office, such as those that were serving in the current FDNG legislative bloc. The URNG saw itself as the vanguard and instead prioritized candidates based upon how much they had contributed to the war effort.[31] The ANN/URNG eventually expelled the FDNG. It is possible that had the URNG worked more closely with the FDNG and taken advantage of its electoral and legislative experience, however limited, it might have won additional congressional seats and mayors in 1999.

The ANN/URNG's performance was also undermined because of its limited relationship with organized civil society. As a result, the URNG could count on few noncombatant supporters in the post-war period. During the war, each time the Guatemalan government's repression intensified against non-revolutionary movements, those who became radicalized sought protection with the guerrillas.[32] Some sympathetic to their cause estimate that the guerrillas counted on the support of up to one million active supporters in the late 1970s and early 1980s. But the relationship between insurgents and mass movements remained much weaker than the relationships that had developed between the insurgents and mass movements in neighbouring El Salvador and Nicaragua. In the early 1980s, the Guatemalan military decapitated the mass-based organizations' leadership and inflicted deep losses upon the rebels. When the military turned over power, at least in name, to a civilian government in 1985, many re-emerging civil society leaders were former guerrillas who had concluded that military victory was impossible and that they had more to gain by finding space within the emerging democratic system.[33] Unlike parties on the right with ties to the oligarchy or military, the URNG as a leftist party with few financial resources depended upon voluntary mass-based support.

The URNG's inability to maintain unity among its former political-military organizations also undermined its electoral performance. Following the height of the violence, former rebels joined opposition political parties and civil society organizations. Other insurgents quit during the negotiations, including the URNG's entire Political-Diplomatic Commission in 1996, to protest against social and economic policies agreed to by the URNG. The wartime divisions weakened the URNG but it still managed to finish third in coalition in 1999. Unfortunately, for the URNG, the divisions that existed during the war and its first electoral contest would prevent them from improving upon their performance in 2003.

Many on the left believed the EGP's Morán was the individual most capable of maintaining unity among the revolutionary left and bridging the gap with the non-revolutionary left.[34] The continuity of the commanders from each organization from the war to the post-war and the agreement forged by Morán guaranteeing that no commander would seek public office might have maintained a unified party but, unfortunately, Morán died in 1998. ORPA's Asturias would have been next in line, but he and his organization, not the entire URNG, were implicated in an embarrassing kidnapping scandal during the latter stages of the peace process. Asturias removed himself from the public face of the URNG and was not even present for the signing of the peace accords. Morán's death and Asturias's isolation disrupted the balance within the URNG's constituent organizations. The URNG's efforts to build a political party that did not have a single individual at the helm, similar to most other Guatemalan political parties, ended in failure.

The FAR's Monsanto became the leader of the URNG upon Morán's death. The FAR was the URNG's third-largest organization after the EGP and ORPA. After losing out for the position of the Secretary General to ORPA's Asturias in August 2001, Monsanto resigned from the party in May 2002 alongside nearly 200 URNG members. Among other issues, the FAR was uncomfortable with ORPA's closeness to Portillo's (FRG) administration.[35] The divisions that occurred within the URNG during and after the peace negotiations and the subsequent party switching (a process known as *transfugismo*) resulted in former combatants running for office with parties from the extreme left to the extreme right, undermining the URNG's argument that it was a party distinct from those already in existence. It is quite possible that former guerrillas participating in a number of parties in 1999 might have confused or dismayed voters; no doubt, it did little to help the URNG's electoral prospects. A larger party might have been able to overcome these challenges, but the URNG was relatively weak, making it extremely difficult to overcome the obstacles. In 2003, the ORPA-dominated URNG competed against Monsanto's FAR-dominated ANN. The ANN actually did much better than the URNG in the legislative elections primarily due to the presence of the popular human-rights advocate Nineth Montenegro at the head of its congressional candidates. Prior to the 2007 elections, the URNG and ANN engaged in a series of talks in which they addressed the possibility of an alliance. However, the ANN preferred to open the alliance to candidates who were anti-oligarchy but not necessarily leftist whereas the URNG preferred leftist and anti-oligarchic.[36] The

URNG was also uncomfortable with the presence of former military officials within the ANN.

While it is plausible that the inability of the URNG to establish and maintain strong relations with a political wing and sectors of organized civil society and to maintain unity hurt its electoral prospects, the effects are more difficult to measure empirically. As mentioned earlier, the URNG called for an alliance that would have brought together former guerrillas (now in different political parties), the FDNG, and other organized groups sympathetic to its revolutionary goals. Unfortunately, the alliance fractured when the FDNG left the ANN. The FDNG and the ANN then ran separate slates of candidates at each level of office.

To what extent did the collapse of the alliance hurt the ANN/URNG in the 1999 elections? By most indicators, the fracturing had very little impact at the presidential level, but an underappreciated effect on legislative elections. In the first round of the presidential elections, the ANN won 12.4% and the FDNG 1.28%. The two candidates who advanced to a second round captured 48% and 30% of the vote; in all likelihood, the ANN/URNG with the FDNG still would have finished a distant third. Following the first round of the 1999 presidential election, the URNG was positioned to help determine the outcome of the second round. However, the ANN/URNG decided not to support either candidate and had little influence on the outcome. It is possible that without the 12% received by the ANN/URNG, one of the two largest parties might have secured a first-round victory instead of advancing to a run-off. The ANN/URNG's ability to influence the electoral outcome in 1999 should have elevated the party to a more prominent position in Guatemalan politics but the URNG failed to take advantage of the situation in 2003, 2007, and 2011, even though each was decided in a second round. It is no guarantee, however, that short-term political influence would have helped the URNG in the long run. Therefore, there is little evidence that electoral rules requiring the winning candidate to surpass 50% of the vote helped the URNG.

For congressional elections, the ANN/URNG captured nine seats with 8% of the vote while the FDNG failed to win a seat, capturing only 2.87% of the national vote. However, if the FDNG had remained part of the ANN/URNG coalition, it is possible that the larger coalition would have picked up an additional five seats, finishing with 14. I assess the extent to which this fracturing affected the URNG by simulating the electoral results that the group would have achieved had the ANN and FDNG presented a single slate of candidates. The larger coalition might have picked up additional seats in Chimaltenango, Sololá, Alta Verapaz, and Petén and one on the national list, a 55% increase in its seat total. Seats in these multimember districts are sometimes decided by hundreds of votes, which magnified every misstep as the ANN/URNG and FDNG competed for support among the same pool of left-leaning voters. The inability of the FDNG and the URNG to maintain an electoral alliance in 1999 was a lost opportunity for the Guatemalan left.

Congressional elections use PR where voters cast separate ballots for the department in which they live and a nationwide district. Under this system, the URNG captured nine seats in 1999 (or 8% of the congress's 113 seats) with 11% of the national vote. To get a handle on how electoral rules affected the URNG's performance in elections for the congress, I simulated the election's outcome had the URNG's votes been translated into seats under an alternative formula for translating votes into seats. Table 3 presents the electoral results for the URNG in the 1999 elections under D'Hondt and the

FROM BULLETS TO BALLOTS

Table 3. 1999 legislative election results for URNG in Guatemala, actual versus simulated.

Department	ANN coalition (actual)	ANN w/ FDNG (simulated)	Seats under D'Hondt (actual)	Seats under LR (simulated)
Central District	1	1	1	1
Guatemala	1	1	1	1
Sacatepéquez	0	0	0	0
Chimaltenango	0	1	0	1
El Progreso	0	0	0	0
Escuintla	0	0	0	1
Santa Rosa	0	0	0	0
Sololá	0	1	0	0
Totonicapán	0	0	0	1
Quetzaltenango	1	1	1	1
Suchitepéquez	0	0	0	0
Retalhuleu	0	0	0	0
San Marcos	1	1	1	1
Huehuetenango	1	1	1	1
Quiché	1	1	1	1
Baja Verapaz	0	0	0	0
Alta Verapaz	1	2	1	1
Petén	0	1	0	0
Izabal	0	0	0	1
Zacapa	0	0	0	0
Chiquimula	0	0	0	0
Jalapa	0	0	0	0
Jutiapa	0	0	0	0
District Deputies	7	9	7	11
National Deputies	2	4	2	2
Total	9	14	9	13

largest-remainder electoral formula used in neighbouring El Salvador where the FMLN had recently competed. D'Hondt tends to reward larger political parties whereas the largest-remainder formula tends to be more favourable to smaller parties.

Under the D'Hondt system, the URNG captured nine seats; seven from district lists and two from a single national list. Simulating the URNG's performance under the largest-remainder formula, the party would have won an additional four seats for a total of 13, picking up additional seats in Chimaltenango, Escuintla, Totonicapán, and Izabal. While 13 would still leave the URNG in third place, an increase of four seats would have been 44% greater than its actual result. A more successful initial performance might have helped maintain unity and attracted additional supporters. While there is no doubt that the URNG entered the 1999 election in a weakened position, the electoral rules worked against them to an extent not appreciated before.

Conclusion

After performing relatively well in its first post-war electoral contest, the URNG lost momentum and has remained a minor political party ever since. Its minor-party status has been based upon several organizational factors and adverse institutional rules. First, the URNG had relatively few combatants and noncombatants supporters at the end of the war. The URNG had been militarily isolated, if not defeated, at the time of its inception as political party. One cannot discount how the death of so

85

FROM BULLETS TO BALLOTS

many mid-level political cadres and leftist intellectuals during the war impacted its electoral fortunes.

Second, the URNG did not maintain a relationship with a political wing during the war. As a result, the URNG was unable to promote its vision of an alternative society to a larger domestic and international audience, one reason why the Guatemalan civil war received comparatively less coverage compared to the wars in Nicaragua and El Salvador even though it was more intense. The closest relationship the URNG developed with a political wing occurred shortly before its insertion into electoral politics but the URNG and FDNG failed to maintain an alliance for even a single election. As a consequence, the URNG failed to capitalize on the FDNG's experience. The inability to present a single slate of candidates in the 1999 elections most likely cost the left several congressional seats.

Third, the URNG has been unable to develop a broad-based alliance with sympathetic groups in civil society. The democratic left rejected such an alliance because they felt that the URNG had tried to impose their candidates and policy preferences in 1999. Partially as a result, the URNG has been unable capitalize electorally on citizen mobilization, particularly Maya mobilization of the last decade over such issues as mining and hydroelectric projects, indigenous rights, corruption, and transitional justice.[37]

Fourth, the URNG was unable to maintain its unity during and after the war. Former rebels left to join opposition political parties, direct civil society groups, and pursue other opportunities well before the end of the war. Several militants grew frustrated with the level of secrecy in negotiations between the commanders and the government and were outraged to learn of elements of the accords, especially when it came to socioeconomic and human-rights agreements. By the first election in which the URNG competed, former guerrillas represented parties across the political spectrum. To many Guatemalan voters, the URNG was no different from other political parties.

The URNG entered the post-war period in a relatively weak position. It had few combatants while those that it did have lacked the financial and technical resources to further the interests of the organization. The URNG failed to convince those who at one time had been involved in the struggle to return to the party or join in an electoral alliance and to maintain unity among its four component organizations. Instead, they ended up competing against each other for the same pool of left-leaning voters, wasting resources, and losing seats in congressional and local elections. Compared to Guatemala's other political parties, the URNG has a sophisticated platform and permanent organizational presence throughout much of the country.[38] In general, the URNG has also promoted more indigenous and female candidates compared to the other parties. However, these advantages have been of little use in attracting large numbers of voters in a candidate-oriented political system where parties capture votes through various clientelistic practices. And while the URNG has a relatively comprehensive party platform, it has, at times, been criticized for producing an outdated platform that did not resonate with what some consider a rather conservative country. Approximately 50% of Guatemalans self-identify as centrist and the percentage who identify as left is double the percentage who identify as right so it is unclear how much that is the case.[39] The URNG also has had difficulties sharing its platform with citizens because of high illiteracy rates, limited media penetration of the countryside, and the fact that some two dozen languages are spoken throughout the country.[40]

Finally, institutional factors played a more important role than previously acknowledged. In terms of legislative elections, the URNG competed under relatively favourable

PR rather than SMD electoral rules. However, the URNG might have been helped had seats been distributed using the largest-remainder formula, where it would have captured four more seats than under the existing D'Hondt formula. Though the electoral formula did not determine outright success or failure, the URNG would have been helped significantly with a change in the electoral rules. Electoral rules are less likely to have such an effect on larger rebel groups. However, every little detail matters for smaller rebel groups, such as the URNG, attempting the transition to political party. Given that some viewed the URNG's performance with nine seats as a failure, 13 seats might have provided the URNG with a greater opportunity to build on this performance in 2003. It might even have changed the future of the left in post-war Guatemala.

Disclosure statement

No potential conflict of interest was reported by the author.

Funding

This work was supported by J. William Fulbright Grant [grant number 49422376].

Notes

1. Allison, "Transition from Armed Opposition"; Allison, "The Legacy of Violence"; Deonandan et al., *Revolutionary Movements*; Manning, "Constructing Opposition in Mozambique"; Manning, "Armed Opposition Groups into Political Parties"; Zeeuw, *From Soldiers to Politicians*; Söderberg-Kovacs, *From Rebellion to Politics*; Longo and Lust, "The Power of Arms".
2. Figueroa Ibarra and Martí y Puig, "Guatemala"; Martí y Puig, "The Adaptation of the FSLN".
3. Garcé, "Ideologías políticas y adaptación partidaria."
4. Allison, "The Legacy of Violence".
5. Wood, "Social Processes of Civil War".
6. Wickham-Crowley, *Guerrillas and Revolution in Latin America*.
7. Ryan, "The Impact of Democratization"; Shugart, "Guerrillas and Elections".
8. Stedman, "The End of the Zimbabwean Civil War"; Stedman, "Spoiler Problems in Peace Processes"; Atlas and Licklider, "Conflict Among Former Allies after Civil War Settlement".
9. Kenny, "Structural Integrity and Cohesion"; Allison and Martín, "Unity and Disunity".
10. Allison, "Transition from Armed Opposition".
11. Shugart and Carey, *Presidents and Assemblies*; Jones, "Presidential Election Laws and Multipartism."
12. Duverger, *Political Parties*; Taagepera and Shugart, *Seats and Votes*; Lijphart, *Electoral Systems and Party Systems*; Lijphart, *Patterns of Democracy*; Hug, *Altering Party Systems*.
13. Madhav, "Inclusive Institutions."
14. Lijphart, *Patterns of Democracy*, 153; see also Taagepera and Shugart, *Seats and Votes*, 133–5.
15. Sánchez, "Guatemala's Party Universe"; Sánchez, "Party Non-Systems".
16. The New Nation Alliance lost its legal standing after the 2007 election but quickly renewed itself as the New Nation Alternative shortly afterwards.
17. Author interview with José Carlos Sanabria, Guatemala, 14 August 2013.
18. Spence et al., *Promise and Reality*, 11.
19. Le Bot, *La Guerra en Tierras Mayas*; Perera, *Unfinished Conquest*; Kruijt, *Guerrillas*.
20. Author interview with Tania Prado Palencia, Guatemala, 19 April 2004.
21. Luciak, *After the Revolution*, 24.
22. Spence et al., *Promise and Reality*; Stanley and Holiday, "Broad Participation, Diffuse Responsibility", 447.
23. Author interview with Alberto Ramírez Recinos, Guatemala, 13 April 2004.

FROM BULLETS TO BALLOTS

24. Bornschein, *Las Izquierdas en Guatemala*.
25. Jaramillo, "Guatemala: Los 'Excommandantes'"; author interview with Rodrigo Asturias, Guatemala, 22 April 2004; author interview with Wilson Romero, Guatemala, 4 July 2007; Bornschein, *Las Izquierdas en Guatemala*.
26. Jonas, *The Battle for Guatemala*.
27. Dunkerley, *Power in the Isthmus*, 491–2.
28. Sichar, *Historia de los Partidos Políticos Guatemaltecos*, 80.
29. Stanley and Holiday, "Broad Participation, Diffuse Responsibility", 435.
30. Figueroa and Martí, "Guatemala."
31. Author interview with Tania Prado Palencia, Guatemala, 19 April 2004.
32. Brockett, *Political Movements and Violence*, 117.
33. Author interview with Tania Prado Palencia, Guatemala, 19 April 2004.
34. Author interviews with Juan Francisco García, Guatemala, 14 April 2004; Tania Prado Palencia, Guatemala, 19 April 2004; Pablo Ceto, Guatemala, 30 July 2013.
35. Author interview with Pablo Monsanto, Guatemala, 8 July 2013.
36. Ibid.
37. Author interview with Pablo Ceto, 30 July 2013; Vogt, "The Disarticulated Movement".
38. Author interview with Marco Barahona, Guatemala, 2 July 2010.
39. Azpuru et al., *Political Culture of Democracy*, 211–13.
40. Viscidi, "The Guatemala Elections".

Bibliography

Allison, Michael E. "The Transition from Armed Opposition to Electoral Opposition in Central America." *Latin American Politics and Society* 48, no. 4 (2006): 137–162.

Allison, Michael E. "The Legacy of Violence on Post-Civil War Elections: The Case of El Salvador." *Studies in Comparative International Development* 45, no. 1 (2010): 104–124.

Allison, Michael E., and Alberto Martín Alvarez. "Unity and Disunity in the Frente Farabundo Martí para la Liberación Nacional (FMLN)." *Latin American Politics and Society* 54, no. 4 (2012): 89–118.

Atlas, Pierre M., and Roy Licklider. "Conflict among Former Allies after Civil War Settlement: Sudan, Zimbabwe, Chad, and Lebanon." *Journal of Peace Research* 36, no. 1 (1999): 35–54.

Azpuru, Dinorah with Juan Pablo Pira and Mitchell Seligson. *Political Culture of Democracy in Guatemala and the Americas, 2012: Towards Equality of Opportunity*. Nashville and Guatemala City: Vanderbilt University, USAID and ASIES, 2012.

Bornschein, Dirk. *Las Izquierdas en Guatemala*. Guatemala: D.R. Fundación Friedrich Ebert, 2000.

Brockett, Charles D. *Political Movements and Violence in Central America*. New York, NY: Cambridge University Press, 2005.

Deonandan, Kalowatie, David Close, and Gary Prevost, eds. *From Revolutionary Movements to Political Parties*. New York, NY: Palgrave MacMillan, 2007.

Dunkerley, James. *Power in the Isthmus*. New York, NY: Verso, 1988.

Duverger, Maurice. *Political Parties: Their Organization and Activity in the Modern State*. New York, NY: John Wiley & Sons, Inc., 1954.

FROM BULLETS TO BALLOTS

Figueroa, Carlos Ibarra, and Salvador Martí Puig. "Guatemala: From the Guerrilla Struggle to a Divided Left." In *From Revolutionary Movements to Political Parties*, edited by Kalowatie Deonandan, David Close, and Gary Prevost, 43–64. New York, NY: Palgrave MacMillan, 2011.

Garcé, Adolfo. "Ideologías políticas y adaptación partidaria: el caso del MLN-Tupamaros (1985–2009)." *Revista de ciencia política (Santiago)* 31 (2011): 117–137.

Hug, Simon. *Altering Party Systems: Strategic Behavior and the Emergence of New Political Parties in Western Democracies.* Ann Arbor, MI: The University of Michigan Press, 2001.

Jaramillo, Velia. "Guatemala: Los 'Excommandantes' se dividen en la política." *Proceso*, México November 4, 2003.

Jonas, Susanne. *The Battle for Guatemala: Rebels, Death Squads, and U.S. Power.* CO: Westview Press, 1991.

Jones, Mark P. "Presidential Election Laws and Multipartism in Latin America." *Political Research Quarterly* 47 (1994): 41–57.

Kenny, Paul. "Structural Integrity and Cohesion in Insurgent Organizations: Evidence from Protracted Conflicts in Ireland and Burma1." *International Studies Review* 12 (2010): 533–555.

Kruijt, Dirk. *Guerrillas: War and Peace in Central America.* London: Zed Books, 2008.

Le Bot, Yvon. *La guerra en tierras mayas.* México: Fondo de Cultura Económica, 1995.

Lijphart, Arend. *Electoral Systems and Party Systems: A Study of Twenty-Seven Democracies, 1945–1990.* Oxford: Oxford University Press, 1994.

Lijphart, Arend. *Patterns of Democracy: Government Forms and Performance in Thirty-Six Countries.* New Haven, CT: Yale University Press, 1999.

Longo, Matthew, and Ellen Lust. "The Power of Arms: Rethinking Armed Parties and Democratization Through the Palestinian Elections." *Democratization* 19, no. 2 (2012): 258–285.

Luciak, Ilja A. *After the Revolution: Gender and Democracy in El Salvador, Nicaragua, and Guatemala.* Baltimore, MD: The Johns Hopkins University Press, 2001.

Madhav, Joshi. "Inclusive Institutions and Stability of Transition Toward Democracy in Post-Civil War States." *Democratization* 20, no. 4 (2013): 743–770.

Manning, Carrie. "Constructing Opposition in Mozambique: Renamo as Political Party." *Journal of Southern African Studies* 24, no. 1 (1998): 161–189.

Manning, Carrie. "Armed Opposition Groups into Political Parties: Comparing Bosnia, Kosovo, and Mozambique." *Studies in Comparative International Development* 39, no. 1 (2004): 54–76.

Martí Puig, Salvador. "The adaptation of the FSLN: Daniel Ortegás Leadership and Democracy in Nicaragua." *Latin American Politics and Society* 52, no. 4 (2010): 79–106.

Perera, Victor. *Unfinished Conquest: The Guatemalan Tragedy.* Oakland, CA: University of California Press, 1993.

Ryan, Jeffrey J. "The Impact of Democratization on Revolutionary Movements." *Comparative Politics* 27 (1994): 22–44.

Sánchez, Omar. "Guatemala's Party Universe: A Case Study in Under-institutionalization." *Latin American Politics and Society* 50, no. 1 (2008): 123–151.

Sánchez, Omar. "Party Non-Systems: A Conceptual Innovation." *Party Politics* 15, no. 4 (2009): 487–520.

Shugart, Matthew Soberg. "Guerrillas and Elections: An Institutionalist Perspective on the Costs of Conflict and Competition." *International Studies Quarterly* 36 (1992): 121–152.

Shugart, Matthew Soberg and John M. Carey. *Presidents and Assemblies: Constitutional Design and Electoral Dynamics.* New York, NY: Cambridge University Press, 1992.

Sichar, Gonzalo. *Historia de los Partidos Políticos Guatemaltecos: Distintas siglas de (casi) una misma ideología.* 2a ed. Guatemala: Editorial Nojib'sa, 1999.

Söderberg-Kovacs, Mimmi. *From Rebellion to Politics: The Transformation of Rebel Groups to Political Parties in Civil War Peace Processes.* PhD diss, Uppsala University, 2007.

Spence, Jack, David R. Dye, Paul Worby, Carmen Rosa de Leon-Escribano, George Vickers, and Mike Lanchin. *Promise and Reality: Implementation of the Guatemalan Peace Accords.* Brookline, MA: Hemisphere Initiatives, 1998.

Stanley, William, and David Holiday. "Broad Participation, Diffuse Responsibility: Peace Implementation in Guatemala." In *Ending Civil Wars: The Implementation of Peace Agreements*, edited by Stephen John Stedman, Donald Rothchild, and Elizabeth M. Cousens, 421–462. Boulder, CO: Lynne Rienner Publishers, 2002.

Stedman, Stephen John. "The End of the Zimbabwean Civil War." In *Stopping the Killing: How Civil Wars End*, edited by Roy Licklider, 125–163. New York, NY: New York University Press, 1993.

Stedman, Stephen John. "Spoiler Problems in Peace Processes." *International Security* 22, no. 2 (1997): 5–53.

Taagepera, Rein, and Matthew Shugart. *Seats and Votes: The Effects and Determinants of Electoral Systems*. New Haven, CT: Yale University Press, 1989.

Vinegrad, Anne. "From Guerrillas to Politicians: The Transition of the Guatemalan Revolutionary Movement in Historical and Comparative Perspective." In *Guatemala after the Peace Accords*, edited by Rachel Sieder, 207–227. London: University of London; Institute of Latin American Studies, 1998.

Viscidi, Lisa. "The Guatemalan Elections." *Counterpunch*, 11 October, 2013.

Vogt, Manuel. "The Disarticulated Movement: Barriers to Maya Mobilization in Post-Conflict Guatemala." *Latin American Politics and Society* 57, no. 1 (2015): 29–50.

Wickham-Crowley, Timothy P. *Guerrillas and Revolution in Latin America: A Comparative Study of Insurgents and Regimes Since 1956*. Princeton, NJ: Princeton University Press, 1992.

Wood, Elisabeth Jean Wood. "The Social Processes of Civil War: The Wartime Transformation of Social Networks." *Annual Review of Political Science* 11, no. 1 (2008): 539–561.

Zeeuw, Jeroen de, ed. *From Soldiers to Politicians: Transforming Rebel Movements after Civil War*. Boulder, CO: Lynne Rienner Publishers, 2007.

Rebel-to-political and back? Hamas as a security provider in Gaza between rebellion, politics and governance

Benedetta Berti[a] and Beatriz Gutiérrez[b]

[a]Institute for National Security Studies, Tel Aviv University, Tel Aviv, Israel; [b]Department of Law, European University of Madrid, Villaviciosa de Odón, Spain

ABSTRACT
After winning the 2006 Palestinian Legislative Council (PLC) elections and subsequently taking control of the Gaza Strip in the summer of 2007, the Palestinian Hamas – a hybrid political, social and military actor – undertook a complex process to ascertain authority and control over Gaza. The article focuses on understanding Hamas's performance as a political party and a "rebel government" as well as the impact of this newly acquired role on the group's strategy. Relying on primary sources, field-work and interviews with members of the Hamas government and its security sector, the study looks at Hamas's role as a security provider and analyses the complex relationship between the institutionalized security sector and the group's insurgent armed wing. Examining Hamas's logic as a security provider and exploring the inherent tensions between political and insurgent logics allows for a better understanding of both the rebel group's role as a political actor and the broader challenges behind the successful rebel-to-political transformations of non-state armed organizations. In doing so it contributes to the emerging literature on non-state actors' shifts between ballots and bullets and on their potential role as alternative governance providers.

Squaring the circle? Rebel groups as political parties and governance-security providers

An especially interesting, yet under-researched question in the emerging literature examining rebel-to-political transformations of non-state armed groups (NSAGs)[1] pertains to these actors' ability to operate as political and governance actors *whilst* retaining a military apparatus.[2] How does preserving an armed wing affect armed groups' operations as political parties and their broader relationship with institutional politics and the existing political order? Even though disarmament and demobilization are often seen as preconditions to rebel party-building,[3] rebel groups can develop political and governance functions while maintaining formal or informal involvement in insurgency and rebellion. Better understanding this dynamic and the inherent tensions it produces can help shed light on the broader challenges of transitioning from bullets to ballots and from war-making to state- and peace-making. Similarly, it can contribute to the weighty debate examining under what circumstances rebel-turned-political groups can become agents of stability or democracy.[4]

The present study examines how a complex NSAG, Hamas, balances "ballots and bullets" by assessing the group's political and governance record through its performance as a security provider. The research is based on field-work in the Gaza Strip (mostly Gaza City) in January 2014. The data were collected through semi-structured interviews with relevant stakeholders from the Hamas government and security sector. Interviewees are fully identified except when they explicitly requested to have their name withheld.

Hamas is especially interesting because it is a *sui generis*, hybrid organization that blurs the lines between insurgent and conventional tactics in its military strategy. It also merges extra-institutional and institutional politics through its activism as a grass-roots socio-political movement and a political party. Finally, Hamas in Gaza de facto challenges the boundaries between state and non-state actor. Indeed, Hamas's political role in the Strip can be seen through the lens of "rebel governance" – "the development of institutions and practice of rule to regulate the social and political life of civilians by an armed group".[5] This concept is especially useful to look at how, when centralized and formal state authority is missing or insufficiently strong, alternative providers of governance emerge to either supplement or replace the state altogether.[6]

Rebel groups' strength as political actors and governance providers can be assessed as a function of their ability to make "collectively binding rules to hierarchically coordinate the provision of common goods"[7] (legal or prescriptive sovereignty)[8] and by their capacity to hold a monopoly on the use of force (effective or material sovereignty). In examining Hamas's record in balancing political and governance imperatives and armed struggle, the research looks especially at Hamas's ability to effectively exercise as well as legitimize a monopoly on force in the Gaza Strip after the group assumed its control in 2007.

This is because the monopoly on the "legitimate use of physical force" resulting in the "capacity to unilaterally impose and enforce collectively binding decisions against the resistance of those who oppose them"[9] is a core attribute of statehood and effective sovereignty. What is more, the exclusive use of collective force is not just necessary to project authority and ensure control over the civilian population, but it should also be seen as a key political tool to build legitimacy. The ability to enforce law and order can be rightfully assumed as the acid test of governance, according to the principle of *salus populi suprema lex*[10] and to the notion of security as a primary public good that "helps to constitute the very idea of 'publicness'".[11]

Effective law-enforcement and provision of security can increase the civilian population's acceptance of the rebel government, thus maximizing trust and quasi-voluntary compliance and allowing NSAGs to rely on more than just coercion – itself organizationally and politically costly – to rule.[12] Kilcullen's theory of competitive control stresses the importance of security as a key step in "creating a normative system that makes people feel safe through the predictability and order that it generates".[13]

In other words, a non-state actor's ability to provide security for the population and territory it seeks to control should not just be seen as a measure of its coercive power. Even though security is indeed related to what Mann calls "despotic power" – the state's control over its citizens – it also reflects the NSAG's "infrastructural power" – the capacity to "penetrate and centrally coordinate the activities of civil society through infrastructure",[14] and it can assist to boost the group's discursive power. A functioning security sector serves indeed a key role in the symbolic politics domain, by allowing a non-state actor to closely mimic and reproduce the language, symbols and structure of a state – as an additional way to gain legitimacy.

Of particular significance, yet under-explored in the literature, is the relationship between a rebel group's efforts to operate in the institutional political domain by becoming in charge of statutory security provision and its competing activities as an insurgent actor.

Accordingly, Hamas – the "Islamic Resistance Movement" (*Harakat al Muqawama al-Islamiyya*) – offers an especially interesting case to examine both the effectiveness and legitimacy of NSAGs as security providers and how the challenges of controlling a dual institutional-insurgent armed apparatus affect the group's ability to balance between "ballots and bullets". Since 2007, Hamas has heavily invested in building a shadow security sector – defined as "all state organizations which are legitimized to use or threaten the use of force in order to protect society and the liberty of its citizens".[15] But has the group's parallel existence as a rebel group compromised its ability to provide security, stability and good governance?

To answer this question, the study first examines Hamas's organizational evolution and transformation into a political party and a *sui generis* rebel government. It then zooms in on understanding what organizational shifts and external policies the group adopted to balance domestic provision of security and external armed struggle. Based on this analysis, the article assesses the success of Hamas's transformation as a dual political-insurgent actor through the lens of its ability to provide security. Finally, in the concluding section, the article relies on Hamas's case to reflect on the broader role of disarmament in rebel-to-political transformations of NSAG as well as on their potential to be agents of stability and democratization. In doing so it contributes to the emerging literature on non-state actors' shifts between ballots and bullets and on their potential role as alternative governance providers.

Hamas: from anti-systemic actor to "hybrid" political party and institutional player in Gaza (2007–2014)

Since its initial creation as the armed wing of the Gaza branch of the Muslim Brotherhood in 1987, the Palestinian Islamic Resistance Movement has been characterized by high internal dynamism and fast-paced change.

At the military level, the group evolved from being a relatively unsophisticated violent faction that relied on individual stabbings against Israelis to becoming a well-trained and organized armed group capable of deadly suicide bombings and of launching rockets deep into Israel. What is more, both during Operation Cast Lead (2008–2009) and even more recently in the course of Operation Protective Edge (2014), Hamas demonstrated its transformation into a "hybrid" actor with high combat skills and focused on engaging its enemy through both classic guerrilla and terrorist tactics such as ambushes, improvised explosive devices (IEDs) and suicide missions as well as by employing more conventional stand-off tactics.

Hamas's military evolution has been mirrored by an even more profound social and political transformation, with the group shifting from the margins to the centre of the Palestinian political stage. This process was accelerated following the group's creation of a political party in 2004 and its victory in the 2006 Palestinian Legislative Council (PLC) elections.[16] After failing to create a unity government with its historical political foe Fatah,[17] simmering tensions between the parties turned into open armed confrontation, culminating with Hamas assuming control of the Gaza Strip in the summer of 2007 and becoming its sole and uncontested ruler.[18]

After 2007 Hamas claimed to have the *de jure* legitimacy on the basis of its 2006 electoral victory and asserted the takeover was due to Fatah being "unwilling to accept the results of Palestinian democracy and the ballot box".[19] Palestinian President and Fatah leader Mahmoud Abbas rejected this interpretation and reacted by dismissing the Hamas-led government and creating a parallel one in the West Bank, producing a schism within the Palestinian political system. The international community supported Abbas by dealing with the Fatah-led Palestinian Authority (PA) as the legitimate government, and rejecting Hamas's claims.

Despite the lack of international recognition Hamas moved ahead with its state-building project and invested in ensuring total control over the Strip while attempting to keep the political system and the economy afloat. It did so facing complex challenges, including the deep enmity of the Fatah-led government in Ramallah as well as an internationally supported Israeli policy of isolation of the Strip – resulting in sharp restrictions in access and exit of goods and people and withholding of international aid as well as tax and custom revenues.

By ruling Gaza, Hamas further transitioned from being a rebel, anti-systemic group into a hybrid armed-political organization involved simultaneously in institutional politics and governance as well as in extra-institutional armed struggle. This process was accompanied by increased tensions between the needs of Hamas as the "resistance" (*Muqawama*) and its broader ethos[20] – calling for sustained confrontation against Israel – and the priorities of Hamas as a political party and a "ruler" – urging the group to take a more risk-averse position and to focus on internal power consolidation. Within Hamas, the at times diverging strategies of governance and armed struggle also led to increased organizational tensions between the group's political, military and external leadership clusters.[21]

To better grasp the inherent tensions between the governance and resistance imperatives as well as the role of security provision as a state-building tool, it is especially interesting to understand both how Hamas reformed the security apparatus in Gaza after 2007 and how it managed the dual insurgent-institutional force structure.

Insurgent and institutional forces in Gaza: an overview of the post-2007 reforms

Following its takeover of the Gaza Strip in June 2007, Hamas found itself operating as the sole political authority in Gaza and managing both "resistance" and security through its armed wing – the Izz al-Din al-Qassam Brigades (Qassam Brigades or IDQB) – and a newly established security sector.

One of the immediate effects of the Hamas takeover was the separation of Palestine into two distinct centres of power, respectively the PA in the West Bank – led by Mahmud Abbas and Fatah – and the Hamas-led government in Gaza. In the Strip, this meant the almost immediate collapse of the security sector, as the security forces on the PA's payroll were ordered not to report for work. In an interview with the authors, Dr. Islam Shahwan, spokesperson of the Hamas Ministry of Interior, described

FROM BULLETS TO BALLOTS

this as a significant challenge due to the sudden quantitative decrease of the security sector from over 50,000 to just 7000 employees.[22]

To cope with this challenge, Hamas relied on its own "Executive Force" (EF) to provide security in Gaza. The EF or *Tanfithya* had been created by Hamas in April 2006, following failed attempts by the Hamas government and Minister of Interior Said Siam to wrestle control of the PA security forces away from the Presidency and Mahmoud Abbas.[23] Even though Abbas had initially banned the EF, Hamas continued to build it up, going from 3000 to 6000–7000 members between its creation and June 2007. The group heavily recruited EF members from both the Qassam Brigades and Hamas's neighbourhood vigilante groups while placing the new force under the control of former Hamas military commander Abu Ubayda al-Jarrah.[24] Before the take-over Hamas attempted to provide the EF with an aura of legitimacy by relying on uniforms and insignia to brand it as an official statutory branch of the PA aimed at curbing crime and disorderly conduct in the Strip.[25] These efforts suggest that even before 2007 Hamas focused on the provision of security as a tool to gain domestic legitimacy and to brand itself as a capable governance actor. In other words, the creation and development of the EF was not just about exercising coercive power, but it rather represented an attempt to further transition from insurgent to institutional stakeholder.

To assist the EF in the immediate aftermath of the takeover Hamas also relied on the Izz al-Din al-Qassam Brigades, directly blurring the lines between internal and external security tasks and between governance and "resistance". Yet, at least formally, this situation was short-lived as by October 2007 the Hamas government in Gaza restructured the security apparatus, dissolved and integrated the EF and created a formal separation between institutional and insurgent forces.[26]

In re-structuring the security forces, Hamas implemented far-reaching changes, placing all the departments previously under presidential control under the Ministry of Interior and downsizing the entire security sector to roughly 15,000 employees.[27] These initial reforms were carried out with the cooperation of veteran and well-respected Fatah police officer Tawfiq Jabr, who had accepted the role of police commander.[28] The reformed security forces were restructured as the Civil Police; the Palestinian National Security Forces (PNSF), in charge of border security; the Security and Protection Apparatus, focusing on protecting key personnel and infrastructure; the Internal Security, tasked with counter-intelligence and preventing Israeli operations inside Gaza; and the Civil Defence Department, dealing with disaster management and response.[29]

The Civil Police – in charge of ensuring law and order in Gaza – lays at the core of Gaza's reformed security sector. Its tasks included road traffic control, crime prevention and prosecution, drugs control, patrolling and crowd control, among others.[30] The police was first developed after the 2007 takeover and subsequently rebuilt after the 2009 Israeli Operation Cast Lead, which heavily targeted the civil police and its infrastructure. During Cast Lead, both the Minister of Interior, Said Siam, and the police commissioner, Tawfiq Jabr, were killed, the latter in an attack on the police academy's graduation ceremony.[31]

Newly appointed Interior Minister Fathi Hammad picked up the pieces in the spring of 2009. In the same period, the Hamas government also invested in establishing a Police College to address the shortage in human resources and to offer specialized training.[32] In parallel with the college, the Ministry of Interior established a Training and Administrative Development department, tasked with organizing courses for its employees as well as with partnering with other ministries and local (and, when possible international) NGOs,[33] and investing in research and development.[34] This is in addition to the Arafat Police Academy, which existed before the 2007 takeover.

Beside the civil police, the other main branch of the security sector, the PNSF, was tasked with protecting the border, preventing smuggling and trafficking, and regulating "suspicious behaviour" along the border area.[35] In an interview with the authors, Eng. Jobeer Dahman, a Captain in the PNSF, emphasized the civilian nature of the PNSF and its mandate.[36] In a separate interview, Sayed Abu Sham'malah, Public Relations and Media Officer of the PNSF, further explained that the PNSF was additionally tasked with implementing orders from the Ministry of Interior aimed at preventing specific groups or individuals from reaching the border areas (for example in the context of the implementation of a ceasefire agreement with Israel, to prevent rogue individuals from launching rockets).[37]

In parallel with these statutory forces, Hamas after 2007 continued to operate through its military wing – the Izz ad-Din al-Qassam Brigades. The IDQB were set up in the early 1990s as a functionally separated and highly secretive wing, in order both to protect it from Israeli security forces attempts to target or infiltrate it and to maximize its freedom of action and flexibility.[38] The group sees itself as part of a "movement of national liberation" and states that its main objective is the liberation of "all Palestine".[39]

While technically subordinated to the Diaspora-based Political Bureau and bound to comply with the directives issued by the group's directive organ, the Shura Council,[40] the IDQB enjoy great tactical freedom and independence.

Operationally, the history of the Qassam Brigades shows remarkable adaptation to its complex combat environment, evolving from conducting relatively unsophisticated acts of political violence in the early 1990s[41] to engaging in large-scale suicide terrorist attacks and, especially since 2005, rocket attacks. After the Israeli unilateral disengagement from Gaza the group focused on qualitative and quantitative growth as well as on boosting its grassroots presence through neighbourhood-based militias aimed at "local community protection".[42] After 2007, the IDQB gained freedom of movement inside the Strip and further evolved towards becoming a quasi-army.[43] They invested in weapon production as well as acquisition, focusing on increasing their artillery capabilities – through rockets and mortars – as well as on anti-tank weapons, IEDs and target-designed explosives, seen as part of the group's effort to prepare for direct engagement with the Israeli Defence Forces (IDF).[44] At the same time, the IDQB's coffers swell through their involvement in Gaza's tunnel economy. Indeed, after 2007 and in order to cope with its isolation, Hamas invested in a sophisticated network of tunnels across the Egyptian border. A vital source of income for Hamas – through taxation – as well as an important means for basic goods to enter Gaza,[45] the tunnels became just as crucial for the IDQB, with the Brigades profiting from their direct involvement in the smuggling business.[46] Hamas's military wing also relied on the underground tunnels to bolster its military apparatus as well as for defensive and, more recently, offensive operations.[47]

With the newly acquired capabilities, the Qassam Brigades began to operate as a de facto army, under the influence of Hezbollah's model of "hybrid warfare" employed during the Second Lebanon War in July 2006. They accordingly organized in divisions, brigades, battalions, platoons and units and partitioned the Gaza Strip territory into military districts, including northern, central and southern sectors as well as a Gaza

City sector, resembling a regular military.[48] Similarly, again in line with the "Hezbollah model", the Qassam Brigades developed both offensive and defensive tasks, with Hamas ground forces targeting the Israeli army within the Strip though hit-and-run operations, ambushes, IEDs and standoff tactics and with the group investing in developing a multi-layered defensive system involving both irregular tactics and semi-conventional combat in urban terrain, including by holding ground.[49]

In terms of tasks, the Qassam Brigades began to represent their mission in line with a regular army's primary function of territorial defence against external threats, also relying on the absence of the Ministry of Defence – itself part of the Oslo framework setting up Palestine as a demilitarized state – to emphasize the separation between the Gaza institutional security sector developed under the Ministry of Interior and the Qassam Brigades.[50] While emerging as an autonomous de facto army, the Qassam Brigades still operate on the basis of the broader ideological concept of "resistance" (*Muqawama*) – a comprehensive framework based on an ethos that emphasizes capacity for sacrifice, ideological purity and a deep sense of individual religious duty. Its translation in military terms generates an operational concept characterized by a willingness to engage in a protracted war to exhaust the enemy as well as in efforts to cause as many casualties as possible and to redirect the struggle to the civilian environment to create moral dilemmas within the enemy. The merging of these operational concepts is clearly reflected the IDQB's statement on the occasion of the 27th anniversary of Hamas's foundation in December 2014, declaring itself to be

> working as the al-Qassam army (…) with its units of mujahideen, which today involve (…) a unit of artillery, an elite unite, a tunnels unit, a snipers unit, an armour unit, an infantry unit and a defence unit to repel further attacks from the Zionist enemy.[51]

Since 2007 the Qassam Brigades' status in Gaza has been highly ambiguous, with the group operating as Gaza's de facto, hybrid, non-institutionalized yet recognized armed forces. Indeed, on the one hand the IDQB focused on external tasks normally associated with a regular army. Unlike a regular army, however, the IDQB were not – formally or informally – taking orders from the Hamas government and did not recognize the group's political leadership as their own superiors. On the other hand, the group was officially recognized – albeit not controlled – by the government and at times it assisted in internal law-enforcement operations. Finally, to make matters even more complicated, double membership between the IDQB and the regular security sector contributed to further blurring the lines between insurgency and governance.

Reconciling bullets and ballots? Hamas's provision of security

There is no question that, after the 2007 takeover of Gaza, Hamas heavily invested in developing both its "rebel forces" – through the IDQB – and the institutional security sector in Gaza. A telling sign of how much the Hamas government cared about its record as security provider is certainly the fact that of the roughly 40,000 employees on Hamas's payroll in 2014 more than 15,000 were part of the security sector.[52]

But how did Hamas fare in terms of effectively providing security? The group's performance in the security realm can be examined by relying on the following parameters, commonly used in the security sector reform and good governance literature:[53]

- monopoly on the use of collective force;

FROM BULLETS TO BALLOTS

- effectiveness of the security sector in providing security;
- level of professionalism and de-politicization and existence of clearly defined roles, rules, procedures and mandates;
- adherence to the rule of law, predictability in administering law-enforcement and justice (fairness) as well as transparency, accountability and clear oversight.

Firstly, monopoly on the use of collective force is a crucial indicator of effectiveness in the provision of security as well as a key measure of effective sovereignty. It is therefore not surprising to note that immediately following the June 2007 takeover Hamas invested greatly in reigning in the public display and use of weapons in Gaza, a move that led the group to directly tackle the previous freedom of action of powerful local clans and families. While this campaign, in addition to a more comprehensive investment in lowering street crime, did significantly increase the Hamas government's level of control over the use of force in the Strip, it still did not resolve the broader issue of how to interact with armed factions operating in Gaza.

Regulation of competing and allied non-statutory "resistance" groups in Gaza created inherent tensions between governance and armed struggle. To dodge this challenge, Hamas adopted a complex approach to "resistance" groups, with the government insisting on the necessity to coordinate armed campaigns against Israel and alternating between openly curbing other armed factions' activities and turning a blind eye and allowing them to operate.[54] At the same time, the Hamas government also clearly stressed that any direct challenge to Hamas's sovereignty over Gaza would be met with armed force to neutralize the perceived threat. A case in point was Hamas's reaction to Jund Ansar Allah's – a Salafi-jihadist group – proclamation of the "Islamic Emirate" of Rafah in August 2009, which led to a swift and brutal crackdown against the group as well as its supporters and leaders.[55]

Hamas's inability to ensure complete monopoly on the use on force transcends the operational level and is intrinsically connected to the group's attempts to balance "resistance" and governance. Indeed, Hamas's need to preserve its parallel armed apparatus as well as its ethos and reputation of "resistance" results in a powerful deterrent against enforcing a zero-tolerance policy with respect to the existence and operation of other armed groups. In turn, this de facto places a constitutive limitation on the rebel government's monopoly on the use of force as well as on its capacity to act as a regular institutional political actor. Of course, the proliferation of armed factions is by no means exclusive to Gaza: competing armed groups also exist in the West Bank, where – unlike the case of Hamas in the Strip – the PA cannot rely on continuous and uncontested territorial control to ensure its sovereignty.[56]

This predicament is also reinforced by the existence of the Qassam Brigades as a highly autonomous and formally separate "non-statutory" group operating in Gaza. This creates a *sui generis* situation where Hamas, the rebel government, shares its monopoly on the use of collective force with the group's military wing. Although the IDQB are part of Hamas and self-identify as an integral part of the organization,[57] their de facto autonomy and independence from the political leadership and the government challenge the latter's exclusive claim to force.

Secondly, Hamas's record as an institutional security provider can be seen as a function of the security sector's ability to preserve law and order in Gaza. One of Hamas's main achievements in the aftermath of the takeover was to quickly reign in crime, unlawfulness and "anti-social behaviour".[58] Beyond the group's obvious interests in exaggerating its own achievements, still – based on both public opinion polls and direct observation – it is possible to affirm that after 2007 the general feeling was that Gaza's streets were generally more secure and that petty crime was more forcefully dealt with (see Figure 1). Interestingly, the general public rate of approval for the Hamas government seems to be influence by the overall perception of security (see Figure 2).

The rise in the public perception of safety is especially important to note because Gaza before 2007 was indeed characterized by a weak and generally ineffective security sector.[59] After 2007, the situation improved, with reported drops in the number of assaults and murders and with a general rise in the number of registered and attended complaints (although the absence of independently verified data on crime rates prevents reporting of more precise numbers).[60] At the same time, the positive impact of the crackdown on crime and lawlessness should also be balanced with the problematic repression of political and civil opposition and growing restrictions in the public sphere.[61]

A third key indicator of an effective security sector is the existence of clearly defined roles, rules, procedures and mandates, along with professionalism and de-politicization. Here, the record is decidedly mixed. On the one hand, one of Hamas's important achievements in reforming the security sector post-2007 was indeed to create an overall more functional and effective structure characterized by clear command and control as well as a formalized division of roles and tasks.

At the same time, the complex and at times blurry relations between the Qassam brigades and the security sector represents the system's Achilles heel. Technically, the IDQB are intended to be completely separate from the institutional security sector. In an interview with the authors, Dr. Islam Shahwan, spokesperson of the Ministry of Interior, asserted that the relationship with the "resistance" is better regulated under the Hamas government than it was before 2007:

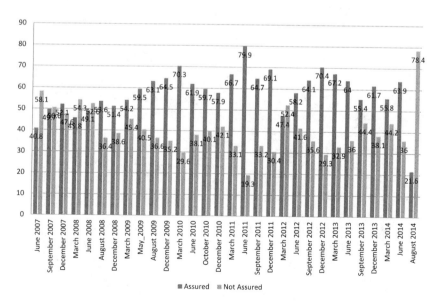

Figure 1. Public perception of security and safety (Numbers given in percentages, dismissing DK/NA values).[77]

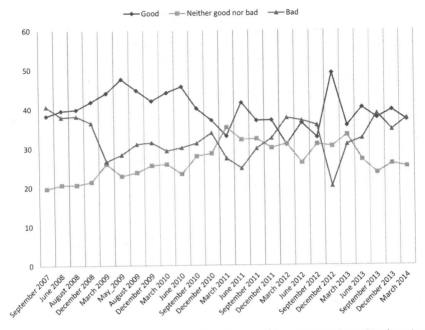

Figure 2. Public perception of the Hamas government's performance between 2007 and 2014 (Numbers given in percentages, dismissing DK/NA values).[78]

Regarding the relations with the resistance movement, previously they had bad relations with the government (...) but nowadays they have very good relationships (...) and they have signed an agreement to define the duties and the tasks and to clarify the roles of both sides (...). The resistance movement is mainly along the borders, to defend the borders and deter the Israelis from an attack; whereas the Ministry of Interior and all its divisions are focused only on internal affairs and on protecting civilians (...).[62]

Yet, reality is more complex. At times the IDQB have carried out domestic law-enforcement, police work or crowd control. Najib and Friedrich explain that the Qassam Brigades after 2007 "have increasingly come to combine paramilitary action with interference in societal affairs",[63] de facto blurring the line between institutional and "resistance" tasks.[64]

Another grey area in terms of blurring the lines between insurgent and institutional forces is the role of the security sector during armed confrontations with Israel as well as its role in enforcing ceasefires. The security sector formally maintains that it does not participate "as per agreement with the resistance" in armed confrontations with Israel.[65] Likewise, the security sector affirms it is not actively involved in issues pertaining to ceasefires with Israel, managed instead by "the different movements involved in the resistance".[66] Reality is more blurry, however, with plenty of room for overlap; for example, security forces arrest individuals who break an agreed lull in hostilities.[67]

In addition, another key shortcoming of the post-2007 security sector is its inability to be de-politicized and bi-partisan. According to the interviews, the legal framework for recruitment should prevent any kind of permeability between members of the "resistance" and the new cadres recruited for the police and security forces. For example, Dr. Ibrahim Habib stated that no former members of the *muqawama* (resistance) groups are allowed to go through the police admission process.[68]

Yet, in practice, dual membership between members of the security sector and both the IDQB and the Palestinian Revolutionary Committees is far from uncommon.[69] What is more, the overall strategy of the Hamas government post-2007 has been in line with appointing supporters and members of the movement to all the main leadership positions in the legislative, judicial and executive branches of government.[70]

Fourthly, an effective security sector can be evaluated on the basis of its adherence to the rule of law as well as on its level of transparency and accountability. The Ministry of Interior as well as the Hamas government in general repeatedly stress the strong focus on meeting international standards in police practices and complying with international law. From within the Hamas ranks, Ghazi Hamad explained: "Transparency in governance is a necessary precondition for accountability."[71]

Still, the security sector's record is far from pristine, as shown by the lack of official data accessible to the public. More substantially, one of the main problems of the post-2007 anti-crime campaign carried out by the security sector is that it was also matched by a crackdown on internal opposition to the Hamas government.[72] Similarly policing has also focused on "social control" and "moral policing", for example by monitoring women's attire or by regulating behaviour deemed as inappropriate.[73]

In parallel, there have also been reports with respect to members of the security sector relying on extra-legal tools and engaging in human rights violations, ranging from abductions, to arbitrary detentions, to unlawful killings, with frequent abuses concerning suspected "collaborators" even as recently as the 2014 war with Israel.[74] In this context, accountability remains an especially opaque issue. This is the case although the Hamas Ministry of Interior has invested in expediting systems to submit citizens' complaints, while also creating human rights units, especially integrated in the Civil Police apparatus (see Supplemental data), and publicizing its desire to cooperate with human rights organizations in Gaza.[75] Still, the inability to obtain independently verified data regarding individual accountability for human rights violations raises serious doubts regarding the actual record when it comes to investigating and punishing those responsible for human rights violations within the security sector (a shortcoming that the Gaza security sector shares with the PA security forces).[76]

Conclusion: rebel-to-political and back?

Hamas, a complex political, social and armed organization involved simultaneously in rebellion, politics and governance, is an interesting case to examine how non-state actors' parallel existence as rebel groups and political parties can affect the transition "from bullets to ballots" and the investments in institutional politics.

A quick overview of Hamas's strategy post-2007 stresses how, without relinquishing its armed wing, Hamas still came to see governance as a core strategic priority. Here, the group used the provision of security as a key tool to boost both its power and its political legitimacy. At the most basic level, investing in security allowed the group to increase its effective control of Gaza and its citizens as well as to rein in competing armed factions and political opponents alike. The provision of security was also a key instrument to strengthen Hamas's claims to legitimacy and "statehood". Indeed, the Hamas government invested heavily in streamlining and reforming Gaza's security sector to increase the level of control and coordination of Gaza's political institutions. In addition, Hamas relied on the performance of the security sector to build legitimacy and project itself as a fully fledged competent, functional and legitimate state. The physical presence and

FROM BULLETS TO BALLOTS

performance of the Hamas-controlled security sector in Gaza represented a powerful visual and symbolic representation of Hamas's state-building. As such, it became key to Hamas's discourse of effective and legitimate sovereignty in Gaza.

At the same time, Hamas's deep investment in the provision of security did not produce a security sector that closely mimics that of a traditional state, but rather a hybrid, *sui generis* force structure along with an ambiguous dual insurgent-institutional apparatus.

On the one hand, some of the main shortcomings of the Hamas security sector – from the failure to tackle the proliferation of armed groups, to the partisan nature of the security sector, to the mixed record in ensuring fairness, transparency and accountability, to the impact of the generally centralizing and authoritarian tendencies of the government – are all shared by the PA security sector in the West Bank and the one in Gaza.

On the other hand, other flaws of the security sector in Gaza, and by extension of Hamas as a security provider, are very much distinctive and embedded in the dual, *sui generis* hybrid existence of Hamas as a political party and a government and as a rebel faction.

Firstly, Hamas's limits in ensuring its monopoly on the use of force are intrinsically connected to the group's attempts to balance "resistance" and governance, a predicament reinforced by the existence of the Qassam Brigades as an autonomous and formally separate "non-statutory" group operating in Gaza, resulting in a hybrid situation where Hamas as a rebel government shares its monopoly on the use of force with the group's military wing.

Secondly, the blurred membership lines between the IDQB and the security sector, and – at times – between the mandate and tasks of institutional and insurgent forces, do affect the security sector's capability to both be de-politicized and to preserve clear and distinct roles and functions amongst its different branches. Finally, this very same blurry situation negatively affects key issues such as transparency or accountability for human rights violations.

These observations are highly pertinent to the broader discussion on the modalities of rebel-to-political transitions in NSAG: they stress how a NSAG's involvement in institutional politics and investment in governance need not necessarily be preceded by disarmament and demobilization of its armed wing. At the same time, the long-term process of socialization and integration into the political system and the future potential for domestic democratization are both significantly complicated by the efforts to reconcile rebellion and institutional politics. In this sense, the tensions inherent within Hamas's quest to be an effective security provider and a "resistance movement" reflect the broader struggle between governance and rebellion and between the competing needs of political accommodation and military struggle faced by non-state armed providers of governance. This reflects the inherent and embedded obstacles of fully transitioning from bullets to ballots, from rebel to institutional political organizations, and from insurgency and war-making to governance and state-making.

Acknowledgements

Most interviews were arranged and coordinated by The House of Wisdom, whose director, Dr. Ahmad Yussef, and Public Relations Officer, Mohammad al-Qattawi, the authors want to thank for their valuable assistance.

FROM BULLETS TO BALLOTS

Disclosure statement

No potential conflict of interest was reported by the authors.

Notes

1. Non-state armed groups can be defined as organizations that are armed, willing and capable to use force to attain their political, economic or ideological goals and not under the formal or de facto control of a state. International Council on Human Rights Policy, *Ends and Means*.5; Schneckener, *Spoilers or Governance Actors?* 8–9; McHugh and Bessler, *Humanitarian Negotiations with Armed Groups*, 14–16. •
2. Some notable exceptions include Van Engeland and Rudolph, *From Terrorism to Politics*; Weinberg et al., *Political Parties and Terrorist Groups*; Martin, "Dilemmas of "Going Legit"; *Armed-Political Organizations*.
3. Manning, "Party-Building on the Heels of War"; de Zeeuw, *From Soldiers to Politicians*.
4. Boudreau, "Security and Democracy".
5. See Mampilly, *Rebel Rulers*; and Mampilly, *Rebel Governance*, 44.
6. Risse, *Governance Configurations*, 3.
7. Börzel *Governance with/out Government*, 8.
8. Asbach, *Sovereignty between Effectiveness*, 2.
9. Börzel *Governance with/out Government*, 13.
10. Literally, "The Well-being of the People is the Supreme Law."
11. Loader and Walker, *Civilizing Security*, 8.
12. Willms, *Justice through Armed Groups*, 24.
13. Kilkullen, *Out of the Mountains*, 114.
14. Mann, *The Autonomous Power*, 188. Quoted in Agnew, *Sovereignty Regimes*, 443.
15. Born and Fluri, *Conclusions*, 104.
16. Turner, "Building Democracy"; Longo and Lust, "The Power of Arms".
17. Al-Arabiya, فتح و حماس توقعان
18. See Berti, *Non-State Actors*.
19. Rabbani, "The Making of a Palestinian Islamist Leader", 70.
20. Sadiki, *Reframing Resistance*, 358–361.
21. Aviad, *Hamas's Military Wing*, 6–7.
22. Interview by the authors with Dr. Islam Shahwan, spokesperson of the Ministry of Interior, Gaza Strip, January 16th, 2014.
23. Cavatorta and Elgie, *The Impact of Semi-Presidentialism*, 35.
24. Sayigh, *Inducing a Failed State*, 20; Cavatorta and Elgie, *The Impact of Semi-Presidentialism*, 50–51.
25. Milton-Edwards, *Order Without Law?*, 665, 671.
26. Sayigh, *Policing the People*, 6; 16–17.
27. Pelham, *How Islamists Govern*, 7.
28. Sayigh, *Policing the People*, 15.
29. Interview, Dr. Islam Shahwan.
30. Interview by the authors with Lieutenant Colonel Mr. Ayoub Abu Sha'ar, Police Spokesperson, Gaza City, Gaza Strip, 21 January 2014.
31. Human Rights Watch, *Precisely Wrong*, 6–7.
32. Interview by the authors with Dr. Ibrahim Habib, Vice-Dean for Academic Affairs, Civil Police Academy, Gaza City, Gaza Strip, 18 January 2014.
33. Interview, Dr. Islam Sahwan; Sayigh, *We Serve the People*, 63–64.
34. Interview by the authors with Eng. Jobeer Dahman, Captain in the Palestinian National Security Forces, Gaza City, Gaza Strip, 20 January 2014.
35. Interview by the authors with Col. Mr. Sayed Abu Sham'malah, Public Relations and Media Officer, Palestinian National Security Forces, Gaza City, Gaza Strip, 20 January 2014.
36. Interview, Eng. Jobeer Dahman.
37. Interview, Col. Mr. Sayed Abu Sham'malah.
38. Kurz and Nahman, *Hamas: Radical Islam*, 16–18; Mishal and Sela, *The Palestinian Hamas*, 173; Gunning, *Hamas in Politics*, 115.

FROM BULLETS TO BALLOTS

39. Brigades of Martyr Izz ad-Din al-Qassam website. http://www.alqassam.ps/arabic/#!/منـذ/

40. Mishal, *The Pragmatic Dimension*, 582; Gunning, *Hamas in Politics*, 98–99.

41. See Berti, *Armed-Political Organizations*, 82–83.

42. Sayigh, *Policing the People*, 46.

43. Interview by the authors with retired high officer Israeli Defence Forces, Herzliya, 10 February 2014.

44. "Hamas's Military Buildup in the Gaza Strip."

45. Pelham, *Diary*.

46. Pelham, *Gaza's Tunnel Phenomenon*, 10.

47. Pelham, *Diary*; and ibid.; Aviad, *Hamas's Military Wing*, 8.

48. Interview by the authors with reservist in the Nahal Brigade, Israel Defence Forces. Tel Aviv, 3 February 2014.

49. Johnson, *Hard Fighting*, 116–119, 140–141; Cohen, *Hamas in Combat*, 7–11

50. Interview J.D., officer in the National Security Forces in Gaza Strip, 17 February 2014.

51. "كتائب القسام, البيانات العسكرية, "خطاب القسام في الذكرى 27 لانطلاق حماس [Brigades al-Qassam, Military statements, "Al-Qassam conmemorate 27 anniversary of Hamas institution"]. See http://www.alqassam.ps/arabic/%D8%A8%D9%8A%D8%A7%D9%86%D8%A7%D8%AA-%D8%A8%D9%84%D8%A7%D8%BA%D8%A7%D8%AA-%D8%A7%D9%84%D9%82%D8%B3%D8%A7%D9%85/5221/%D8%AE%D8%B7%D8%A7%D8%A8-%D8%A7%D9%84%D9%82%D8%B3%D8%A7%D9%85-%D9%81%D9%8A-%D8%A7%D9%84%D8%B0%D9%83%D8%B1%D9%89-27-%D9%84%D8%A7%D9%86%D8%B7%D9%84%D8%A7%D9%82%D8%A9-%D8%AD%D9%85%D8%A7%D8%B3.

52. Sayigh, *We Serve the People*, 8; al-Sharq al-Awsat, *Funding Government*.

53. Ignacio Cano, *Policía y su Evaluación*; Caparini and Furi, *Relevance of Democratic Control*, 8; Karkoszka, *The Concept of Security*.

54. International Crisis Group, *Ruling Palestine I*, 8.

55. Al-Jazeera, مقتل زعيم جند انصار

56. Sayigh, *Policing the People*, 25.

57. See http://www.alqassam.ps/arabic/#!/منـذ/

58. Nissenbaum, *Hamas Promotes 'Gaza Riviera'*.

59. Al-Mezan Center for Human Rights, *Jungle of Guns & the Law of the Jungle*, 6–22.

60. Palestinian Civil Police, وزارة الداخلية الفلسطنية ; and Sayigh, *Policing the People*, 59–60.

61. Interview by the authors with civil society activist in Gaza [name/location of the interview withheld], 26 October 2014.

62. Interview, Dr. Islam Shahwan.

63. Najib and Friedrich, *Non-Statutory Armed Groups*, 123.

64. International Crisis Group, *Radical Islam in Gaza*, 9–10.

65. Interview, Dr. Islam Shahwan.

66. Interview by the authors with Eng. Tariq Esawi, Captain in the National Security Forces, Gaza City, Gaza Strip, 20 January 2014.

67. Interview, Eng. Tariq Esawi.

68. Interviews by the authors with Dr. Ibrahim Habib, Vice-Dean in the Gaza Police Academy, Gaza City, Gaza, 18 January 2014, and with Dr. Islam Shahwan.

69. Intelligence and Terrorism Information Center at the Israeli Intelligence Heritage & Commemoration Center (IICC), *Members of Hamas*, 1.

70. Berti, *Non-State Actors*.

71. Hamad, *The Challenge for Hamas*, 134.

72. Interview, civil society activist. Milton-Edwards, *The Ascendance of Political Islam*, 1591; Brown, *Gaza Five Years On*, 5.

73. Sayigh, *Policing the People*, 2; Sayigh, *We Serve the People*, 111.

74. Human Rights Watch, *Under the Cover*; International Amnesty, *Strangling Necks*, and Independent Commission for Human Rights, *The Status of Human Right*, 12.

75. Sayigh, *We Serve the People*, 29–31.

76. Sayigh, *Policing the People*, 19–20.

77. Polls 24 (June 2007)–52 (June 2014), http://www.pcpsr.org/en/node/154, Special Gaza War Poll (August 2014), http://www.pcpsr.org/en/node/492, Palestinian Center for Policy and Survey Research (accessed 10 February 2015).

FROM BULLETS TO BALLOTS

78. Polls 25 (September 2007), 28 (June 2008)–51 (March 2014), Palestinian Center for Policy and Survey Research (http://www.pcpsr.org/en/node/154) (accessed 10 February 2015).

Bibliography

Agnew, John. "Sovereignty Regimes: Territoriality and State Authority in Contemporary World Politics." *Annals of the Association of American Geographers* 95, no. 2 (2005): 437–461.

فتح و حماس توقعان على اتفاق مكة برعاية العاهل السعودي. [Fatah and Hamas sign the Mecca Agreement under the Saudi monarch auspices] al-Arabiya, February 8, 2007. Accessed January 30, 2015. http://www.alarabiya.net/articles/2007/02/08/31472.html.

مقتل زعيم جند انصار الله برفح [Killed leader of Jund Ansar Allah in Rafah], Al-Jazeera, August 15, 2009. Accessed June 15, 2015. http://www.aljazeera.net/news/arabic/2009/8/15/%D9%85%D9%82%D8%AA%D9%84-%D8%B2%D8%B9%D9%8A%D9%85-%D8%AC%D9%86%D8%AF-%D8%A3%D9%86%D8%B5%D8%A7%D8%B1-%D8%A7%D9%84%D9%84%D9%87-%D8%A8%D8%B1%D9%81%D8%AD.

Al-Qassam Brigades. البيانات العسكرية, "خطاب القسام في الذكرى 27 لانطلاقة حماس" [Military Statements: Commemorating the 27th anniversary of Hamas institution], December, 14th, 2014.

al-Sharq al-Awsat. *Funding Government Proving Tough: Hamas*, December 24, 2010.

Amnesty International. *"Strangling Necks". Abductions, Torture and Summary Killings of Palestinians by Hamas Forces during 2014 Gaza/Israel Conflict.* London: Amnesty International, 2015.

Asbach, Olaf. "Sovereignty between Effectiveness and Legitimacy Dimensions and Actual Relevance of Sovereignty in Bodin, Hobbes and Rousseau." *Eurostudia. Revue Transatlantique de Recherche sur l'Europe* 2, no. 2 (2006). Accessed January 30, 2015. http://www.cceae.umontreal.ca/EUROSTUDIA-Transatlantic-Journal,671.

Aviad, Guy. "Hamas's Military Wing in the Gaza Strip: Development, Patterns of Activity and Forecast." *Military and Strategic Affairs* 1, no. 1 (2009): 3–15.

Berti, Benedetta. *Armed-Political Organizations: from Conflict to Integration.* Baltimore, MA: John Hopkins University Press, 2013.

Berti, Benedetta. "Non-State Actors as Providers of Governance: The Hamas Government in Gaza between Effective Sovereignty, Centralized Authority, and Resistance." *Middle East Journal* 69, no. 1 (2015): 9–31.

Born, Hans, and Philipp Fluri. "Conclusions." In *Security Sector Reform and Democracy in Transitional Societies*, edited by Hans Born, Marina Caparini and Philipp Fluri, 103–105. Geneva Centre for the Democratic Control of Armed Forces. Baden-Baden: Nomos Verglagsgesellschaft, 2000.

Börzel, Tanja A. *Governance with/out Government. False Promises or Flawed Premises? Governance in Areas of Limited Statehood - New Modes of Governance?* Working Paper Series, No. 23. Berlin: Research Center (SFB) 700, 2010. Accessed January 30, 2015. http://www.sfb-governance.de/en/publikationen/working_papers/wp23/SFB-Governance-Working-Paper-23.pdf#.

Boudreau, Vincent. "Security and Democracy: Process and Outcome in a New Policy Context." *Democratization* 14, no. 2 (2007): 313–330.

FROM BULLETS TO BALLOTS

Brown, Nathan. "Gaza Five Years On: Hamas Settles In." *Middle East Papers*, Washington DC: Carnegie Endowment for International Peace, 2012.

Cano, Ignacio. *La Policía y su Evaluación. Propuestas para la Construcción de indicadores de Evaluación en el Trabajo Policial*. Santiago de Chile: Centro de Estudios para el Desarrollo. Accessed January 30, 2015. http://www.iidh.ed.cr/comunidades/seguridad/docs/seg_docpolicia/la%20policia%20y%20su%20evaluacion.pdf.

Caparini, Marina, and Philip Furi. "The Relevance of Democratic Control and Reform of the Security Sector." In *Security Sector Reform and Democracy in Transitional Societies*, edited by Hans Born, Marina Caparini and Philipp Fluri, 8–11. Geneva Centre for the Democratic Control of Armed Forces. Baden-Baden: Nomos Verglagsgesellschaft, 2000.

Cavatorta, Francesco, and Robert Elgie. "The Impact of Semi-Presidentialism on Governance in the Palestinian Authority." *Parliamentary Affairs* 63, no. 1 (2010): 22–40.

Cohen, Yoram. *Hamas in Combat. The Military Performance of the Palestinian Islamic Resistance Movement*. Policy Focus no. 97. Washington, DC: Washington Institute for Near East Policy, 2009.

DCAF. *Towards Palestinian National Reconciliation*. Reference Texts. Geneva: DCAF, 2011.

Gunning, Jeroen. *Hamas in Politics: Democracy, Religion, Violence*. London: Columbia University Press, 2008.

Hamad, Ghazi A. "The Challenge for Hamas-Establishing Transparency and Accountability." In *Entry-Points to Palestinian Security Sector Reform,* edited by Roland Friedrich and Arnold Luethold, 131–144. Geneva: Geneva Centre for the Democratic Control of Armed Forces, 2007.

عريقاتَ. الرئيس عباس سيكلف حماس تشكيل الحكومة الفلسطينية الجديد [Erekat: The president Abbas will set Hamas to form a new Palestinian government], Al-Ayyam, January, 27th, 2006. Accessed January 30, 2015. https://www.alyaum.com/article/2352867.

حكومة حماس 2006 [Hamas Government 2006], Al-Arabiya, March 26th, 2006. Accessed January 30, 2015. http://www.alarabiya.net/views/2006/03/29/22382.html.

Human Rights Watch. *Precisely Wrong: Gaza Civilians Killed by Israeli Drone-Launched Missiles*. New York: Human Rights Watch, 2009.

Human Rights Watch. *Under the Cover of War*. New York: Human Rights Watch, 2009.

Independent Commission for Human Rights. *The Status of Human Rights in Palestine*. 1 January-31 December 2011. Ramallah: Independent Commission for Human Rights, 2012.

IICC (Intelligence and Terrorism Information Center at the Israeli Intelligence Heritage & Commemoration Center). *Members of Hamas' Internal Security Services Who Were Also Operatives in Hamas' Military-Terrorist Wing and Were Killed in Operation Pillar of Defense, 2012*. Accessed January 30, 2015. http://www.terrorism-info.org.il/Data/articles/Art_20445/E_255_12_214222039.pdf.

IICC. *Hamas's Military Buildup in the Gaza Strip*, 2008. Accessed January 30, 2015. http://www.terrorism-info.org.il/Data/pdf/PDF1/hamas_080408_501786899.pdf

International Council on Human Rights Policy. *Ends and Means: Human Rights Approaches to Armed Groups*. Versoix, 1995. Accessed January 30, 2015. www.ichrp.org/files/reports/6/105_report_en.pdf.

International Crisis Group. *Radical Islam in Gaza*. Middle East Report 104. Brussels: International Crisis Group, 2011.

International Crisis Group. *Ruling Palestine I: Gaza under Hamas*. Middle East Report 73. Brussels: International Crisis Group, 2008.

Johnson, David E. *Hard Fighting: Israel in Lebanon and in Gaza*. Santa Monica: RAND Corporation, 2011. Accessed January 30, 2015. http://www.rand.org/pubs/monographs/MG1085.html.

Karkoszka, Andrzej. *The concept of Security Sector Reform*. Geneva: Centre for the Democratic Control of Armed Forces. Accessed January 30, 2015. www.dcaf.ch/content/download/35997/527211/file/Karkoszka.pdf.

Kilkullen, David. *Out of the Mountains: The Coming Age of the Urban Guerrilla*. Oxford: Oxford University Press, 2013.

Kurz, Anat, and Tal Nahman. *Hamas: Radical Islam in a National Struggle*. Memorandum No. 48. Tel Aviv: Jaffee Center for Strategic Studies, 1997.

Loader, Ian, and Neil Walker. *Civilizing Security*. Oxford: Oxford University Press, 2007.

Mampilly, Zachariah. *Rebel Rulers: Insurgent Governance and Civilian Life during War*. Ithaca: Cornell University Press, 2011.

Longo, Matthew, and Ellen Lust, "The Power of Arms: Rethinking Armed Parties and Democratization through the Palestinian Elections." *Democratization* 19, no. 2 (2012): 258–285.

Mampilly, Zachariah. "Rebel Governance and the Syrian War." In *The Political Science of Syria's War*, edited by the Project on Middle East Political Science (POMEPS), 44–47. Washington, DC, 2013. Accessed January 30, 2015. http://pomeps.org/wp-content/uploads/2013/12/POMEPS_BriefBooklet22_PoliSciSyria_Web.pdf.

Mann, Michael. "The Autonomous Power of the State: Its Origins, Mechanisms and Results." *European Journal of Sociology* 25, no. 2 (1984): 185–213.

Manning, Carrie. "Party-Building on the Heels of War: El Salvador, Bosnia, Kosovo and Mozambique." *Democratization* 14, no. 2 (2007): 253–272.

Martin, Susanne. "Dilemmas of "Going Legit": Why Should Violent Groups Engage in or Avoid Electoral Politics?." *Behavioral Sciences of Terrorism and Political Aggression* (2013). doi:10.1080/19434472.2013.834375.

McHugh, Gerard, and Manuel Bessler. *Humanitarian Negotiations with Armed Groups. A Manual for Practitioners.* New York: United Nations Office for the Coordination of Humanitarian Affairs (OCHA), January 2006. Accessed January 30, 2015. https://docs.unocha.org/sites/dms/Documents/HumanitarianNegotiationswArmedGroupsManual.pdf.

Milton-Edwards, Beverly. "The Ascendance of Political Islam: Hamas and Consolidation in the Gaza Strip." *Third World Quarterly* 29, no. 8 (2008): 1585–1599.

Milton-Edwards, Beverly. "Order without Law? An Anatomy of Hamas Security: The Executive Force (Tanfithya)." *International Peacekeeping* 15, no. 5 (2008): 663–676.

Mishal, Shaul, and Avraham Sela. *The Palestinian Hamas. Vision, Violence and Coexistence.* New York: Columbia University Press, 2006.

Mishal, Shaul. "The Pragmatic Dimension of the Palestinian Hamas: A Network Perspective." *Armed Force & Society* 29, no. 4 (2003): 569–589.

Najib, Mohammad, and Roland Friedrich. "Non-Statutory Armed Groups and Security Sector Governance." In *Entry-Points to Palestinian Security Sector Reform*, edited by Roland Friedrich and Arnold Luethold, 103–130. Geneva: Geneva Centre for the Democratic Control of Armed Forces, 2007.

Nissenbaum, Dion. "Hamas Promotes 'Gaza Riviera'." *Edmonton Journal*, July 29, 2007 (accessed January 30, 2015) [LexisNexis].

Palestinian Civil Police. [وزارة الداخلية الفلسطينية بعد عام تقضي على الفلتان وتفرض الامن والأمان رغم الحصار The Interior Minister eliminates the chaos and imposes safety and security after a year despite the blockade] July 2008. Accessed January 30, 2015. http://www.police.ps/ar/news-action-show-id-884.htm

Pelham, Nicolas. "Diary: How to Get by in Gaza." *London Review of Books* 31, no. 20 (2009): 36–37.

Pelham. "Gaza's Tunnel Phenomenon: The Unintended Dynamics of Israel's Siege." *Journal of Palestine Studies* XLI, no. 4 (2012): 6–31.

Pelham, Nicolas. "How Islamists Govern: Lessons from Gaza." *TIDA Synthesis Report*, Gaza, January 2011.

Podder, Sukanya. "Mainstreaming the Non-State in Bottom Up State-Building: Linkages between Rebel Governance and Post-Conflict Legitimacy." *Conflict, Security & Development* 14, no. 2 (2014): 213–243.

Rabbani, Mouin. "The Making of a Palestinian Islamist Leader: Interview with Khalid Mishal: PART II." *Journal of Palestine Studies* 37, no. 4 (2008): 59–81.

Risse, Thomas. *Governance Configurations in Areas of Limited Statehood. Actors, Modes, Institutions, and Resources, Governance in Areas of Limited Statehood - New Modes of Governance?* Working Paper Series, No. 32. Berlin: Research Center (SBF) 700, 2012. Accessed January 30, 2015. http://www.sfb-governance.de/en/publikationen/working_papers/wp32/SFB-Governance-Working-Paper-32.pdf#.

Sadiki, Larbi. "Reframing Resistance and Democracy: Narratives from Hamas and Hezbollah." *Democratization* 17, no. 2 (2010): 350–376.

Sayigh, Yezid. "Inducing a Failed State in Palestine." *Survival* 49, no. 3 (2007): 7–40.

Sayigh, Yezid. "Policing the People, Building the State: Authoritarian Transformation in the West Bank and Gaza," *Middle East Papers*, Washington DC: Carnegie Endowment for International Peace, 2011.

Sayigh, Yezid. "We Serve the People. Hamas Policing in Gaza." *Crown Paper 5.* Waltham: Crown Center For Middle East Studies, 2011.

FROM BULLETS TO BALLOTS

Schneckener, Ulrich. *Spoilers or Governance Actors? Engaging Armed Non-State Groups in Areas of Limited Statehood.* Governance in Areas of Limited Statehood - New Modes of Governance, Working Paper Series, no. 21. Berlin: Research Center (SFB) 700, 2009. Accessed January 30, 2015. http://www.sfb-governance.de/en/publikationen/working_papers/wp21/SFB-Governance-Working-Paper-21.pdf

Turner, Mandy. "Building Democracy in Palestine: Liberal Peace Theory and the election of Hamas." *Democratization* 13, no. 5 (2006): 739–755.

Van Engeland, Anisseh, and Rachel M. Rudolph. *From Terrorism to Politics.* Aldershot, England: Ashgate, 2008.

Weinberg, Leonard Ami Pedahzur, and Arie Perliger. *Political Parties and Terrorist Groups.* London: Routledge, 2008.

Willms, Jan. *Justice through Armed Groups' Governance-An Oxymoron?.* Governance in Areas of Limited Statehood - New Modes of Governance, Working Paper Series, no. 40. Berlin: Research Center (SFB) 700, 2012. Accessed January 30, 2015. http://www.sfb-governance.de/en/publikationen/working_papers/wp40/SFB-Governance-Working-Paper-40.pdf#.

de Zeeuw, Jeroun J. *From Soldiers to Politicians: Transforming Rebel Movements after Civil War.* Boulder: Lynne Reinner, 2007.

Index

Note: **Bold face** page numbers refer to figures and tables. Page numbers followed by "n" refer to endnotes.

Abbas, Mahmoud 94, 95
African Democracy Encyclopaedia 27
Albizures, Miguel Angel 82
Allison, Michael 2, 24
ANC in South Africa 35
anti-social behaviour 98
anti-systemic group 93 -4
AOGs *see* armed opposition groups
Arafat Police Academy 96
armed groups, post-war political incorporation, of: analysis 13–15; data analysis 11–13; dataset 10–11, 16n3; descriptive statistics **12**; party formation **13**; party history 6–7; post-war environment 9; prior electoral experience 14; war duration 15; war legacies 7–8; war to peace transition 8–9
armed opposition groups (AOGs) 6, 10–11, 14–16
Arzú, Alvaro 75
Asturias, Rodrigo 79, 82, 83

Barrios, Walda 79
Batta, Anna 24, 59
bayto 64
Berger, Oscar 77, 79
Berti, Benedetta 2, 28
Bicesse agreement 30
bi-partisan 100
Birnir, Johanna 44
Burundi: CNDD-FDD in 25; peace agreements 29

Ceto, Pablo 79
Chad, peace agreements 29
CIA World Fact Book 27

CIA-orchestrated coup (1954) 75
Civil Police, Gaza 95–6
civil war: Hamas 91–102; peace after 1, 41–52; peace settlement and 2; political party formation after 4–16; post-war democratization 58–69; rebel-to-party transformations 22–37; resumption 45, 50; URNG 74–87
clandestine political violence 61, 62, 64
classic Maoist-style guerrilla army 64
CLEA Political Parties Dataset 27
Close, David 24
CNDD-FDD *see* National Council for the Defense of Democracy–Forces for the Defense of Democracy
CNDP *see* National Congress for the Defence of the People
Collier, Paul 60
Colom Caballeros, Alvaro 77, 79
Colombian conflict 22
conflict(s) 4–5; armed conflict 5; episode 7, 10–14, 17n30; incompatibility 31; intensity 5, 7, 17n25; post-conflict election 10
congressional elections 84
consensualism 47
Cox estimation techniques 48, 54n56

Dahman, Jobeer 96
De Zeeuw, Jeroen 7, 8, 26, 36
decision-making mechanisms 7
Della Porta, D. 61
demobilization 26, 81, 82, 91, 102
Democratic Convergence 75
Democratic Party 66
Democratic Republic of Congo (DRC) 36
democratization: domestic democratization 102; issue of 1–2; liberal peacebuilding 4; rebel-to-party transformation on 23, 24, 59, 93; *see also* post-war democratization

109

INDEX

_andan, K. D. 24
_e-politicization 98–100, 102
despotic power 92
D'Hondt system 84–5, 87
diaspora-based political party 62, 96
Dodouet 24
Downs, Anthony 3n3, 54n35
Doyle, Michael 8
DRC _see_ Democratic Republic of Congo

Economic Theory, An (Downs) 54n35
EF _see_ Executive Force
EGP _see_ Guerrilla Army of the Poor
EISA _see_ Electoral Institute for Sustainable
    Democracy in Africa
election: as Democratic Convergence 75;
    marginal electoral force 77–81; and
    post-insurgent authoritarian parties
    67–8; violence 10–11
electoral democracy 24, 81
electoral environments 7
Electoral Institute for Sustainable
    Democracy in Africa (EISA) 27
electoral participation 36
electoral rules: disadvantageous 81–5;
    SMD 87
EPL _see_ Popular Liberation Army
Ethiopian People's Revolutionary Democratic
    Front (EPRDF) 32, 60, 62, 66, 68
Ethiopian revolution 62
ethnic fractionalization 47, 52
ethnic mobilization 60
Executive Force (EF) 95

FAR _see_ Rebel Armed Forces
Farabundo Martí National Liberation Front
    (FMLN) 26, 52, 74–6, 81, 82, 85
FARC _see_ Revolutionary Armed Forces of
    Colombia
Fatah-led Palestinian Authority (PA) 94
FDNG _see_ New Guatemala Democratic
    Front
FDR _see_ Salvadoran Democratic
    Revolutionary Front
Fein, Sinn 28
Firm and Lasting Agreement 75
FMLN _see_ Farabundo Martí National
    Liberation Front
former rebel parties: analysis 47–52;
    candidate recruitment of 24, 41; design
    and methodology 45–7; inclusion and
    peace duration 42–5; in national
    government 2; into political process 41

Fortna, Virginia Page 7, 8, 46, 59
Free Aceh Movement (GAM) 25
Freedom House 9, 27
FRG _see_ Guatemalan Republican Front
Friedrich, Roland 100
FSLN _see_ Sandinista National Liberation
    Front

Gaddafi, Muammar 69
GAM _see_ Free Aceh Movement
Gaza: Civil Police 95; Hamas in 93–4;
    institutionalized security sector in 2;
    insurgent and institutional forces
    in 94–7; provision of security 97–101;
    rebel groups 91–3
Gerdes, Felix 24
gimgema 64
"governance without government." 60
governance-security providers, rebel
    groups as 91–3
Grisham, Kevin E. 24
Guatemalan National Revolutionary Unit
    (URNG): demobilization 82;
    disadvantageous electoral rules 81–5;
    legislative election results **85**; marginal
    electoral force 77–81; organizational
    and institutional challenges 75–7;
    Political-Diplomatic Commission 83;
    post-war legislative elections in **80**;
    post-war presidential elections in **78**;
    weak organizational ties 81–5
Guatemalan Republican Front (FRG) 77
Guatemalan Workers' Party (PGT) 74
Guerrilla Army of the Poor (EGP) 74, 79, 83

Habib, Ibrahim 100
Hamad, Ghazi 101
Hamas: anti-systemic actor to "hybrid"
    political party 93–4; _de jure_ legitimacy 94;
    as governance-security providers 91–3;
    human rights violations 101; hybrid
    politico-military organizations 24;
    institutionalized security sector 2;
    military evolution 93; non-statutory
    "resistance" groups 98; as political
    parties 91–3; post-2007 reforms 94–7;
    provision of security 97–101; public
    perception **99, 100**; rebel-to-
    political 101–2
Hammad, Fathi 95
Hampson, Fen O. 43
Hartzell, Caroline 43
Hatz, Sophia 2

110

INDEX

hazard modelling techniques 47–52
Hensell, Stephan 24
Hezbollah 24, 96–7
hinfishfish ("anarchy") 62
Huang, Reyko 7, 8, 59
Huntington, Samuel P. 58
hybrid political party, anti-systemic actor to 93–4
hybrid politico-military organizations 24, 28

IDF *see* Israeli Defence Forces
IDQB *see* Izz al-Din al-Qassam Brigades
IEDs *see* improvised explosive devices
IFES Election Guide *see* International Foundations for Electoral Systems Election Guide
improvised explosive devices (IEDs) 93, 96, 97
IMR *see* Infant Mortality Rate
Indonesia, GAM in 25
Infant Mortality Rate (IMR) 47
infrastructural power 92
insurgent groups: Hamas 2; into political parties 65–6; post-insurgent parties 58–60, 62; as proto-political parties 60–1
International Crisis Group 27
International Foundations for Electoral Systems (IFES) Election Guide 27
Intrastate peace agreements: characteristics **32**; conflict incompatibility **31**; rebel-to-party transformations **33–4**; with/without rebel-to-party provisions **29–31**
Ishiyama, John 2, 7, 14, 24, 59
Islamic Renaissance Party 42
Islamic Resistance Movement 93
Israeli Defence Forces (IDF) 96
Israeli Operation Cast Lead (2009) 95
Izz al-Din al-Qassam Brigades (IDQB) 94–102

Kagame, Paul 60, 62, 63, 65, 67
Kilcullen's theory of competitive control stresses 92
Kosovo Liberation Army (KLA) 25

Lancaster House agreement 32
leadership: of EPRDF 62; of NRA 62; of RPF 63; of victorious insurgent groups 61–3
legislative inclusion 44, 50
legitimate political actor 24
legitimate power-procurement tool 44
Levitsky, S. 59
liberal peacebuilding 4, 25, 59

liberated territory administration 63–5
Licklider, Roy 43
logit model 11–13, 48, **51**, 52
long-term inclusion 41–5, 47
Lopez, Beatriz 2
Lyons, Terrence 1, 2, 59

Mann, Michael 92
Manning, Carrie 2, 24, 27, 52, 59
marginal electoral force 77–81
Marshall, Michael Christopher 2, 24
Marxist-Leninist League of Tigray (MLLT) 62–4
Marxist-Leninist URNG 75
Menkhaus, K. 60
military rule, legacies of 63–5
Ministry of Interior 94–7, 99, 101
MLLT *see* Marxist-Leninist League of Tigray
Monsanto, Pablo 83
Morán 83
Mozambique: peace process 27, 30; Renamo rebel movement in 26, 35, 59
MPLA *see* People's Movement for the Liberation of Angola
multi-party system 23, 60, 76
Museveni, Yoweri 61–3, 67

Najib, Mohammad 100
National Advancement Party (PAN) 77
National Congress for the Defence of the People (CNDP) 36
National Council for the Defense of Democracy–Forces for the Defense of Democracy (CNDD-FDD) 25
National Patriotic Front of Liberia (NPFL) 35
National Resistance Army (NRA) 59, 62–6
National Resistance Movement (NRM) 60–2, 66–8
National Unity of Hope 79
negotiation process 42, 43, 52
neo-patrimonial links 60
New Guatemala Democratic Front (FDNG) 82, 84, 86
Nilsson, Desirée 43
"no party" system 60, 67
non-state armed groups (NSAGs) 26, 27, 34, 91, 103n1
NPFL *see* National Patriotic Front of Liberia
NRA *see* National Resistance Army
NRM *see* National Resistance Movement
NSAGs *see* non-state armed groups

INDEX

..., Thomas 43
..e-party authoritarian regimes 60
Organization of the People in Arms
  (ORPA) 74, 79, 83

PA *see* Fatah-led Palestinian Authority
Palestinian Islamic Resistance Movement 93
Palestinian Legislative Council (PLC)
  elections 93–4
Palestinian National Security Forces
  (PNSF) 95–6
Palestinian Revolutionary Committees 101
PAN *see* National Advancement Party
PARLINE database 46
"party nonsystem" 77
Peace Agreement Dataset 27, 29
peace agreements: characteristics 34;
  intrastate peace agreements **29–31**;
  rebel-to-party outcomes 26–7; rebel-
  to-party provisions 25–6, 28–32;
  rebel-to-party transformations 32–5
"peace and stability committees" 66
Peace Keeping Operation and Performance
  (PKOP) 46
peace settlement 1–2, 4–5, 23, 36, 42–4
"People's Democratic Organizations" 66
People's Movement for the Liberation of
  Angola (MPLA) 32
PGT *see* Guatemalan Workers' Party
PKOP *see* Peace Keeping Operation and
  Performance
PLC elections *see* Palestinian Legislative
  Council elections
PNSF *see* Palestinian National Security
  Forces
political inclusion 44
political life: of civilians 92; during
  wartime 60–1
political party: definition 5, 28; insurgent
  groups into 65–6; rebel groups as 91–3;
  rebel movements into 59–60; strength
  and durability of 58
Political-Diplomatic Commission 83
Popular Liberation Army (EPL) 30
Portillo, Alfonso 77
post-2007 reforms 94–7
post-Cold War era 23, 26, 30, 36
Post-Communist successor parties 7
post-conflict elections 10, 47, 67, 68
post-conflict parties 59
post-conflict peace 1, 43, 53
post-conflict political process: analysis
  47–52; candidate recruitment of 41;

design and methodology 45–7; inclusion
  and peace duration 42–5; large-n
  comparative research on 5; peace
  duration analyses **49**; power sharing
  institutions 43
post-insurgent authoritarian parties 67–8
post-insurgent parties 58, 60, 62, 63
post-rebel party formation: after civil
  war 5–10; analysis 13–15; binary
  variables, marginal effects **13**; data
  analysis 11–13; descriptive statistics **12**;
  logit model **13**; multivariate model 12
post-settlement states 51
post-war democratic institutions 5
post-war democratization 2, 7; elections
  and post-insurgent authoritarian
  parties 67–8; insurgent groups into
  political parties 65–6; liberated territory
  administration 63–5; political life during
  wartime 60–1; rebel movements into
  political parties 59–60; wartime
  institutions 61–3
post-war environment 9
post-war legislative elections, in
  Guatemala **80**
post-war party: centripetal dynamics 59;
  development 7; formation 10
post-war political incorporation, of armed
  groups: analysis 13–15; data
  analysis 11–13; dataset 10–11, 16n3;
  descriptive statistics **12**; party
  formation **13**; party history 6–7;
  post-war environment 9; prior electoral
  experience 14; war duration 15; war
  legacies 7–8; war to peace transition 8–9
post-war political system 1, 2, 5, 9, 41
post-war presidential elections, in
  Guatemala **78**
post-war security 9, 25
power-sharing 26, 34–6, 43
PR *see* proportional representation
Prevost, Gary 24
pre-war experience 6–7, 10
pre-war incarnation, as electoral party 13–14
pre-war politics 5
PRIO Battle-Related Deaths datasets 7
professionalism 98, 99
proportional representation (PR) 9, 14, 76–7
proportionality assumption 48
proto-political parties, insurgents as 60–1

Qassam Brigades *see* Izz al-Din al-Qassam
  Brigades (IDQB)

INDEX

RCs *see* Resistance Councils
Rebel Armed Forces (FAR) 74, 79, 83
rebel groups: definition of 28; as
  governance-security providers 91–3; as
  political parties 91–3; pre-war political
  experience 2; transformation 1–2;
  victory 58–69
rebel organization 41
rebel party-building 91
rebelocracy 63
Rebel-to-Party Dataset 27–8, 32, 35
rebel-to-party transformations 1–2;
  intrastate peace agreements **33–4**; in
  peace agreements 25–36; previous
  research on 23–5
Recinos, Alberto Ramírez 81
Relief Society of Tigray 64
Renamo in Mozambique 35
Renamo rebel movement 59
Resistance Councils (RCs) 64
resistance movement 102
Revolutionary Armed Forces of Colombia
  (FARC) 22
revolutionary brigades 68
Revolutionary United Front (RUF) 25, 35
Romero, Wilson 81
Ross, Michael 47
RPF *see* Rwandan Patriotic Front
RUF *see* Revolutionary United Front
Rwandan Alliance for National Unity 62, 63
Rwandan Patriotic Front (RPF) 60, 62,
  63, 65–6

Salvadoran Democratic Revolutionary
  Front (FDR) 75
Sambanis, Nicolas 8
Sandinista National Liberation Front
  (FSLN) 74
Sandoval, Miguel Ángel 79
Sartori, Giovanni 5, 6
Schoenfeld residual-based test 48
SDS *see* Serb Democrat Party
security sector: functioning 93; Gaza 95,
  97; institutionalized 2; post-2007 99–101
separate peace 9, 15, 16
Serb Democrat Party (SDS) 34
Shahwan, Islam 94, 99
Sham'malah, Sayed Abu 96
short-term inclusion 42
Sierra Leone, RUF in 25, 35
single member district (SMD) voting 76, 87
SMD voting *see* single member district
  voting

Smith, Ian 2
Söderberg Kovacs, Mimmi 2, 24, 26, 43
South West Africa People's Organization
  (SWAPO) 32, 35, 65–6
Suazo, Adan E. 42
suicide missions 93
SWAPO *see* South West Africa People's
  Organization

terrorist organizations 5, 24
Tigray Development Association 64
Tigray People's Liberation Front
  (TPLF) 62–6
Tupamaros 74
Tutsi-dominated RPF 66

UCDP *see* Uppsala Conflict Data Program
Uganda Patriotic Movement 62
Uganda Resistance News 64
Ugandan Patriotic Movement 62
United Nations Peacekeepers (UNPKO) 50
unlawfulness 98
UNPKO *see* United Nations Peacekeepers
Uppsala Conflict Data Program (UCDP):
  Actor Dataset 10–11, 27; Conflict
  Encyclopedia 27; Conflict
  Termination 7, 10–11; Peace Agreement
  Dataset 27, 28–9, 45
Uppsala-PRIO Armed Conflict Data
  Project 45
URNG *see* Guatemalan National
  Revolutionary Unit

Van de Goor, Luc 27
Variance Inflation Factor (VIF) test 48
victorious rebel groups 15, 58–69
VIF test *see* Variance Inflation Factor test
Villagrán, Arnoldo 82

war weariness 8, 47, 51
warlord democrats 24–5
wartime institutions 61–3
"wartime political orders" 61
war-to-peace transition 59, 60, 68
war-weary publics 65
Way, L. 59
weak organizational ties 81–5
Weibull estimation techniques 48
World Bank Data on Human
  Development 47
World Bank Political Institutions Dataset 27

Zenawi, Meles 62, 69